LINGUISTICS & PHILOSOPHY

Edited by

Günther Grewendorf • Wolfram Hinzen
Hans Kamp • Helmut Weiss

Band 3 / Volume 3

Manuel Bremer • Daniel Cohnitz

Information and Information Flow

An Introduction

ontos
verlag
Frankfurt • Lancaster

Bibliographic information published by Die Deutsche Bibliothek
Die Deutsche Bibliothek lists this publication in the Deutsche Nationalbibliographie;
detailed bibliographic data is available in the Internet at http://dnb.ddb.de

North and South America by
Transaction Books
Rutgers University
Piscataway, NJ 08854-8042
trans@transactionpub.com

United Kingdom, Ire, Iceland, Turkey, Malta, Portugal by
Gazelle Books Services Limited
White Cross Mills
Hightown
LANCASTER, LA1 4XS
sales@gazellebooks.co.uk

©2004 ontos verlag
P.O. Box 15 41, D-63133 Heusenstamm
www.ontosverlag.com

ISBN 3-937202-47-1

2004

All rights reserved. No part of this book may be reprinted or reproduced or utilized
in any form or by any electronic, mechanical, or other means, now known or hereafter invented,
including photocopying and recording, or in any information storage or retrieval system,
without permission in writing from the publisher.

Printed on acid-free paper
(TcF-Norm).

Printed in Germany.

Table of Content

Introduction
Varieties of Information   7

1| The Syntactic Approach to Information
   Answering a Question by Decreasing Randomness   13
1|1 The Syntactic Approach to Information I   15
1|2 The Syntactic Approach to Information II   31
1|3 Algorithmic Information Theory   65

2| The Semantic Approach to Information
   What Information is given by that Sentence?   73
2|1 Explicating Information by Possible Worlds   75
2|2 Strong Semantic Information   89
2|3 Do You Get Information in a Logic Course?   94

3| The Causal Approach to Information
   The Information You Have but Do not Believe   109
3|1 The Causal Theory of Information Flow   111
3|2 Information in Externalist Epistemology   124
3|3 Perception, Belief, and the Problem of
     Misrepresentation   135

4| Situation Theory and Information
   Bringing Ontology back into Information Theory   147
4|1 The Framework of Situation Semantics: 149
4|2 Information Architecture and Constraints   163

5| Information Flow in Distributed Systems
   Renaming Your 'Evening Star' Yields New Information   175
5|1 Information Flow within the Situation Framework   177
5|2 Information Flow and Paraconsistency   195
5|3 Get Yourself Involved into Impossible Situations   210

| 5|4 Genetic Information? | 225 |

Epilogue 237
Further References 239
Glossary of Notation 242

Introduction
Varieties of Information

EVERYONE speaks of the age of information. Even though the first hype of the internet has gone, electronic mail and information retrieval have become part of our daily life. But what *is* information?

In his famous popular scientific book *A Brief History of Time*, Stephen Hawking drops the following remark while discussing information and its relation to the entropy of the universe:

> The progress of the human race in understanding the universe has established a small corner of order in an increasingly disordered universe. If you remember every word in this book, your memory will have recorded about two million pieces of information: the order in your brain will have increased by about two million units. (Hawking 1988, 152.)

The quoted passage suggests that progress in understanding is correlated with the amount of information received, that the amount of information received can objectively be measured (is the same for every reader), and – in particular – is a function of the number of words one does remember of the information received. That sounds as if a theory of information is just around the corner, we simply have to put all these quantities together, something Stephen Hawking presumably has done already, how else did he arrive at the numerical values?

But unfortunately things are not that simple. Why should we think that the amount of information or understanding that a reader might gain from reading *A Brief History of Time* is a function of the number of words in it? Consider the speech of a politician or, better, a collection of them. For example, consider the fictive book *Collected Speeches of George W. Bush*. Let us assume that the number of words in it it is by coincidence the same as the number of words in *A Brief*

History of Time, we will assume that even the number of letters is exactly the same. Besides the fact that it is not about the same topic and therefore does not have the same information in it, it is a fair assumption that it will have less information in it on whatever topic it is. The reason is simply the familiar fact that some people might use more words than others to convey the same amount of information, politicians (not only George W. Bush) are infamous for this.

This means that even if the amount of information – for example – in a book is an objective property of the book, it is not clear why it should be a function of the actual number of words or letters in it. Maybe Stephen Hawking could have written an abridged version of the book that told us just as much about the universe and its history as the actual *A Brief History of Time* does. Hm, ...then maybe the amount of information gained by reading *A Brief History of Time* is not a function of the number of words that *A Brief History of Time* is actually composed of, but it rather is a function of the number of words the most abridged version of it would be composed of that still told us the same about the history of the universe. Well ...., not quite. Wouldn't the language matter, the book is written in? Some languages allow for shorter words, phrases and sentences than others do, so it should be in the right language, too, shouldn't it?

Moreover, so far we did not discuss the issue of objectivity that is implied in the quoted passage. Assume that you are a physicist who is almost as smart and knowledgeable as Stephen Hawking is and you are asked to proofread *A Brief History of Time* before it goes into print. Since you might know all the facts about the history of the universe already that are covered in the book, is it plausible to assume that the order in your brain, even if it increased by about two million units, is correlated with an increased understanding of the universe? Probably it is not. It seems that information can also be said to have a subjective component. I learned quite a bit from reading *A Brief History of Time*, somebody with more background knowledge could even have learned more than I did, but somebody with as much background knowledge as Stephen Hawking himself has about the history of the universe, might not learn anything from reading the book, for him it would not be of any informational value.

Or imagine somebody not capable of understanding English, who learns *A Brief History of Time* by heart simply because his TV set broke down and he couldn't think of anything better to do than that. He could remember every word of the book and the order in his brain would have increased by two million units, but he would not have gained any information about the universe. For him the whole book is mere gibberish. This is just like it must be for Stephen Hawking's computer that has the whole book stored on his harddrive. The computer's understanding of the universe did not increase in any way when Hawking wrote the book into it. Is it correct to say that the computer has information about the universe when he is not capable of using it in any way? But then, why do biologists say that genes carry information? Do they only carry it for the biologists who can decode it and use it? Or does the DNA carry the information for the ribosome to put just the right amino acids together to form a particular protein?

So far we have considered information and its relation to symbols, content, languages, background knowledge, and usage. But isn't nformation also connected with truth?

A Brief History of Time makes a number of claims about the history of the universe and future development of physics. Imagine that future reasearch would falsify most, if not all of these claims. Would we still regard *A Brief History of Time* as containing information if what is said in it were false? It seems that only true statements can inform you about anything, but that makes *misinformation* a contradiction in terms, at least if taken to be a species of information.

The questions raised so far do suggest that 'information' is a word with a very broad meaning which is used to describe a variety of different things.

There is a *syntactic* sense, as we found in the quote by Stephen Hawking, in which information is measured via symbols. In this sense my computer receives 200 Mbit of information per second via my broadband internet connection at the moment, while in fact it is receiving only tons of spam emails that are not 'informative' at all.

There is a *semantic* sense, in which information is a matter of the content associated with the words or symbols the information is coded in.

There is an *epistemological* sense, in which information is tied to knowledge and truth and plays an enormous role for organisms like us who can exploit it. How do all these different senses of 'information' belong together?

We need a theory of information. A theory that tells us what information is. A theory that tells us how it works that sentences, utterances, signs are said to carry information. Does not the smoke carry the information that there is a fire nearby? A theory of information should tell us what informational content is and how we arrive at information or use information to get at more information. It should tell us how information flows from some piece of information we got to more information. – That is what this little book is all about.

This book is conceived as an introductory text into the theory of syntactic and semantic information, and information flow. Syntactic information theory is concerned with the information contained in the very fact that some signal has a non-random structure. Semantic information theory is concerned with the meaning or informational content of messages and the like. The theory of information flow is concerned with deriving some piece of information from another.

The book is in part historical. We will start with a comparison of the early syntactical theory of information and the early semantic approach. We present the basic ingredients of the theories so that the concepts of *information* and *amount of information* can be introduced. Explaining the virtues of these approaches we also keep an eye to their shortcomings if not in the theories themselves then maybe with respect to our pre-scientific understanding of what information is. The main part will take us to situation semantics as a foundation of modern approaches in information theory. We give a brief overview of the background theory and then explain the concepts of information, information architecture and information flow from that perspective. This part of the book really presents 'state of the art' theories. Finally we shall discuss the applicability of modern information theory to some practical and philosophical problems.

Almost all chapters are centred on the *basics* of the respective theories. Our aim is to give you an overview with some but not too much technical details and a list of further reading material you might turn to.

Information is a key concept in the cognitive sciences, information science, philosophy of language, and logic. Our intended reader is the undergraduate in one of these disciplines looking for a general account of information that is neither too informal nor too technical.

We presuppose general knowledge (undergraduate level) of First Order Logic, highschool mathematics, and some general knowledge of analytic philosophy of language.

We started this book project from our experience with graduate courses at the University of Düsseldorf and at the European Summer School in Logic, Language and Information 2002 in Trento, since we had the impression that people were looking out for some kind of introductory text to the topic.

Personal pronouns are haphazardly used with no preferences for either sex. Feel free to be upset. We are from Old Europe.

We would like to express our thanks to people who supported our project and helped us to improve our several drafts. These people include: Stefan Bagusche, Marc Breuer, Axel Bühler, Filip Buekens, Luciano Floridi, Phillip Keller, Jochen Lechner, John Perry, Michael Preuss, Markus Werning, the students of our courses in Düsseldorf and Trento, and anonymous referees.

1 | The Syntactic Approach to Information
Answering a Question by Decreasing Randomness

TERRIBLY enough you get a scary letter every other day. You do not know who is sending them. Every letter contains the same message: '1111111'. What does it mean? You have no idea, but every other day there is this letter. Now today something changed. You opened your daily letter and it read '1116111'. You still cannot say what this means, but one thing is for sure: something has changed. The occurrence of this other symbol (the '6') may have some importance, otherwise why should there be the change? Is a threat becoming real? Are your days counted?

In this example we have a letter with no words at all. We could even leave the numerals out and have their work done by some marks on the paper. So we left out conventional meaning. Our first perspective on information is not concerned with (conventional) meaning at all. Words or signs that have meaning obviously seem to carry some information. Does carrying information, however, start only with conventions ruling symbols? Even if we leave out the proverbial black sky giving you information about the storm to come, and deal with written marks or symbols only, can symbols viewed from a merely syntactic perspective carry information? What kind of information would that be? We expect information to be about the world. How could a sign with no meaning carry information about something else?

What *is* important in our story of meaningless signs is the change that occurs between '1111111' and '1116111'.

On the one hand the mere occurrence of change has an epistemic component: You expected your regular letter with only '1's in it. This expectation was frustrated. An expectation being frustrated carries information. You learn, at least, that the world does not follow the simple rules you thought of so far.

On the other hand the sign itself has changed from one that can easily be described as 'a row of seven '1''s' to one that needs a more complex description, like 'three '1's followed by a '6', followed by three '1's'. The second description is more complex. Needing a more complex description the second string is more random. The less randomness we have the easier the rule to describe a string – here we have entered a syntactic perspective on information. You might, further on, think of the programming needed to generate the string: The first string needs a single loop, the second needs more lines of code.

Imagine a little expansion of our story: You are a secret agent and the letter comes from your informant. You and your informant have invented a system of codes corresponding to possible states of affairs of your target site. Given this scheme the sudden occurrence of the '6' might very well carry a lot of information. It may code the delivery of the jewels you have been after the last seven years. Given some predefined question a string of symbols having no conventional meaning (in the strict sense) can carry information about the world. From all the possible symbols that could have taken the place of the '6' (say a '7' for the presence of too much police, a '8' for summoning you back to headquarters etc.) just the '6' occurred. Something from a range of possible answers was singled out – that sounds very much like giving specific information!

1|1 The Syntactic Approach to Information I

The pre-history of Information theory

This book tries to explore the history of the way information is treated in modern philosophy and semantics, especially in situation theory. One of the roots of the modern treatment is surprisingly unphilosophical. It dates back to the old days of the telephone and the engineering problems connected with this technology. But before we turn to the problems early communication engineers had to face, we will go even further back – into the history of thermodynamics.

Entropy, Maxwell's Demon, and Information

Most books and papers on information theory refer to the concept of entropy in thermodynamics and either emphasize that the concept of entropy or information in information theory is relevantly connected with it, or that it most definitely has nothing to do with it:

> [...] The use of the entropy concept [in information theory] is a perfectly valid one. Boltzmann's order-disorder notion is directly applicable to the process of communicating information. (Cherry 1952, 651)

> I find it utterly unacceptable that the concept of physical entropy, hence an empirical concept, should be identified with the concept of amount of semantic information [...]. (Bar-Hillel 1964, 309)

We will briefly discuss what the entropy concept refers to in thermodynamics and how it came to be connected with the concept of information *within* physics. We think that this is of some interest. It is also interesting – from a philosophy of science point of view – to note that a certain mathematical calculus can equally well be at the heart of three (or more) theories with different domains of application.

Disorder

As it was the received view from about the 18th century, the transition from order to disorder is an irreversible process that applies not only to my desk, but also to yours and the whole universe (which is comforting ... at least the part of the story which does not contain the phrase 'terminal heat death' and the like). The idea is that whenever work or kinetic energy is dissipated within a system (e.g. because of friction, deformation, electric resistance, etc.) the disorderly motions of molecules are increased. Equally, whenever substances are mixed, dissolved and diffused with one another, the spatial positions of the molecules are in a less ordered arrangement. This transition from order to disorder that underlies all these kinds of processes, is expressed in thermodynamics by the second law, stating that the entropy of the universe increases. All these processes are irreversible, i.e. in these cases we are unable to change one form of energy back into another (like thermal energy into mechanical energy), an increase of entropy means a decrease of available energy. The irreversibility of these processes is 'what gives time its arrow'. The fact that entropy of the universe increases makes possible to tell whether a movie showing the development of the universe is run backwards or forwards.

In 1871 the Scottish mathematician and physicist James Maxwell designed the following thought experiment to demonstrate the statistical nature of the second law of thermodynamics:

> One of the best established facts in thermodynamics is that it is impossible in a system enclosed in an envelope which permits neither change of volume nor passage of heat, and in which both the temperature and the pressure are everywhere the same, to produce an inequality of temperature or of pressure without the expenditure of work. This is the second law of thermodynamics, and it is undoubtedly true as long as we can deal with bodies only in mass, and have no power of perceiving or handling the separate molecules of which they are made up. But if we conceive a being whose faculties are so sharpened that he can follow every molecule in its course, such a being, whose attributes are still as essentially finite as our own, would be able to do what is at present impossible to us. For we have seen that the molecules in a vessel full of air at uniform temperature are moving with velocities by no

means uniform, though the mean velocity of any great number of them, arbitrarily selected, is almost exactly uniform. Now let us suppose that such a vessel is divided into two portions, A and B, by a division in which there is a small hole, and that a being, who can see the individual molecules, opens and closes this hole, so as to allow only the swifter molecules to pass from A to B, and only slower ones to pass from B to A. He will thus, without expenditure of work, raise the temperature of B and lower that of A, in contradiction to the second law of thermodynamics. (Maxwell 1871)

This thought experiment was intended by Maxwell to dramatize the fact that the second law is a statistical principle and that it is not *certain* that the entropy in any case increases. If Maxwell's demon is not only conceivable but compatible with the rest of thermodynamics, the second law is not a strict law. A decrease of entropy were not physically impossible, but merely too unlikely to occur – a huge difference for the status of the second 'law' of thermodynamics.

The discussion about whether or not the demon really is physically possible turned out to be a discussion about whether or not the increase in entropy caused by the actions of the demon would outweigh the decrease in entropy that would result from his ordering of the molecules. In 1929 though, the discussion started to center around a new concept that found its way into physics, the concept of *information*.

Information and Negentropy

In that year the Hungarian Physicist Leo Szilard directed the attention of his colleagues to the fact that in order to fulfill his task and separate the faster from the slower moving molecules, the demon had to gain and store information about the molecules' speed and position. Thermodynamics would predict that the physical realization of this information processing would increase the entropy sufficiently, but for an 'intelligent being' this could not be proven. Szilard argued instead that an inanimate construction with the necessary abilities could increase the entropy sufficiently. Subsequent discussion like Brillouin's in 1962 and Rodd's in 1963 suggested that the information processing of the demon would definitely outweigh the decrease in entropy the demon could achieve by sorting the molecules and processing the information. Even if a demon existed, the entropy change of the universe would be positive and the second law could not be violated in any way.

This result led to much confusion about the character of information theory. Amount of information was by Brillouin considered to be identical with negentropy (negative physical entropy) (Brillouin 1951), the genius mathematician and physicist Johann von Neumann seems to have identified logic, information theory and thermodynamics (Bar-Hillel 1964, 12; but see also his remarks in Von Neumann 1955, 400), some have considered information theory to be a branch of thermodynamics. Such identifications should of course be taken less seriously. It is one thing to show that the physical realization of the information processing Maxwell's demon has to conduct will necessarily produce an amount of physical entropy in accordance with the second law, quite another to identify the amount of information generated with the thereby generated negentropy.

The philosopher Rudolf Carnap tried to show that there are two quite different concepts of entropy involved, one which is the physical quantity Boltzmann was concerned with, the other a concept of entropy used by Brillouin and others which is a logical or epistemological concept (Carnap 1977).

Carnap did not publish this interesting essay during his lifetime, although it might be the way to clarification in this area. His colleague Bar-Hillel formulated the main idea behind this distinction:

> As I see it, the entropy of a system is a determinate quantity. However, being fallible human beings, we are unable to determine this quantity, at least in general. If the outcome of some action of ours is a function of the entropy of a system, then we would like to act on our knowledge of the true value of this quantity. However, all we can do is to act on our estimate of this value. [...] Now, of course, estimates are relative to available evidence, hence in a sense to the state of knowledge of the estimator. Someone's estimate of the entropy of a given system depends upon his state of knowledge. I would not urge not to formulate this situation by saying that the entropy of the system depends upon his state of knowledge. (Bar-Hillel 1964, 310)

Thus the concept of information and how it is measured plays a certain role in thermodynamics, namely in the discussion of the physical possibility of Maxwell's demon. There is indeed an application where information theory is used to solve a physical puzzle, but this should not lead to the identification of the physical quantity of entropy with information theoretic entropies we will be dealing with in what follows.

Nyquist, Hartley and the birth of MCT

The first thing to note about one of the most important forefathers of information theory, is the awkward story why he has the name he has. In 1880, one year after he had married Katarina Eriksdotter, a certain Lars Johnsson and his brother Olof bought the farm 'Där Sör', 40 kilometers North of Karlstad in Sweden. As it turned out, just hundred meters from their new home lived another Lars Johnsson, which automatically caused a huge problem with the mail delivery. An envelope saying

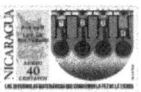

To:
Lars Johnsson
Värmland
Sweden

(Värmland is the name of the region in which 'Där Sör' was situated) couldn't carry enough information for the mailman to know whether he should deliver the letter to Lars on 'Där Sör' or to the other Lars in the immediate neighborhood. The information the mailman received from such an envelope simply did not reduce the possible addressees to one, the intended addressee. But instead of demanding more specific information in the address, like

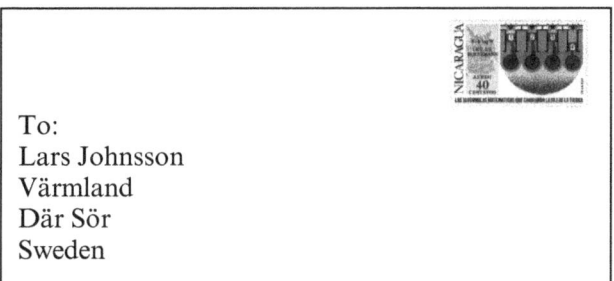

a different solution was chosen, which was not even rare in Sweden at that time: Lars at Där Sör changed his name, from 'Johnsson' into 'Nyquist'. In information theoretic terms that was even pretty efficient. The signal that had to be written on the envelop to carry enough information, viz. who the intended addressee is, did not need to increase (it still contained the same lines as before):

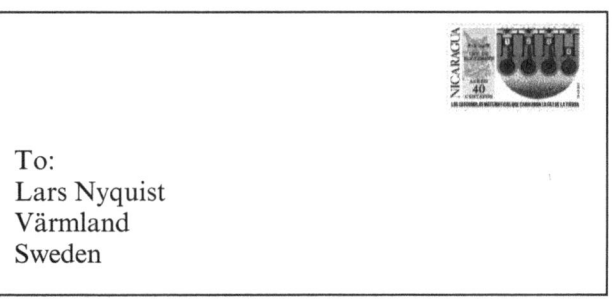

But it now carried enough information for the mailman to know who the intended addressee was. *Why* this was a good way of dealing with the problem is something that the Swedes couldn't know by that time, for one of the men who would provide the basic concepts for the explanation of that was not yet born.

This happened 9 years later. On February 7 1989 Harry Nyqusit, the fourth of eight of John Nyquist's children was born. He is probably one of the most misspelled and mispronounced forefathers of information theory, thanks to Lars Johnsson who lived in the neighborhood of Där Sör.

Writing in 1924, Nyquist's aim was to determine what factors are governing the maximum speed of data transmission in a given communication system. One basic factor determining the speed of transmission is of course the limit imposed on the telephone cable by such factors as power, noise, and the frequency of the signal. Nyquist abstracted away from these limiting factors and considered an ideal cable that is distortionless, in order to inquire what factors are determining communication speed besides power, noise, and the frequency of the signal. Nyquist identified two factors which are determining the speed of transmission in such an idealized system: (i) the shape of the signal and (ii) the code that represents the message. Nyquist argued (i) that signals for the considered telegraph systems are most efficiently transmitted if their carrying waves are rectangular rather than sine shaped. (ii), given the shape of the carrying wave, it is the ideal code which determines the transmission speed. Nyquist was able to measure the amount of 'intelligence' that can be transmitted by the ideal code, by suggesting that the speed of transmission of intelligence is proportional to the logarithm of the number of current values which can be used to codify the message. The notion of an 'ideal code', Nyquist's distinction between the characters of a message and the signal elements representing the characters, his suggestions concerning characters of non-uniform duration, etc. were all of importance for the development of communication theory.

But the even more interesting point of Nyquist's work for us is how he arrived at his measure of information: He started from the assumption that certain factors are relevant for determining the transmission speed and then abstracted away from them, in order to identify the other factors also involved. Thus Nyquist worked backwards, starting from the given transmission speed of a given communication system towards a general account how information can be ideally coded, which is only one step away from measuring the information produced by the source of the communication system.

Another pioneer of Information Theory was Ralph Vinton Lyon Hartley. Hartley was born in Spruce, Nevada on November 30 1888 and was thus just a couple of months older than Nyquist. After his graduation from Oxford he joined the Research Laboratory of the Western Electric Company and worked later (after W.W.I.) for the Bell laboratories.

In the 1928 edition of the *Bell System Technical Journal*, the very same journal in which Nyquist had published his ideas just four years earlier, Hartley published his famous paper 'Transmission of Information', in which he – for the very first time – defined such key notions as 'precision of information' and 'amount of information'. It might well be that Hartley was aware of Nyquist's earlier work, especially since some of Hartley's ideas appear to be shaped by Nyquist's way of dealing with the problem of information, in particular by his explicit assumption that all symbol sequences are of the same length or size. Although this influence is likely, Hartley did not cite Nyquist's work, nor anyone else's work, for that matter.

The topic of Hartley's paper is to set up a quantitative measure whereby various different communications systems may be compared in terms of their capacities to transmit information. Thus Hartley's approach, which is intended to cover telegraphy and telephony, picture transmission and television via wire and radio paths is definitely broader than Nyquist's was, who was only concerned with telegraphy. As well as Nyquist's, Hartley's discussion is directed at an idealized model of a communication system, in order to achieve a general analysis of the factors involved. Hartley is already well aware of the fact that 'information' is a term with a rather broad meaning. Therefore he starts his discussion by considering what factors are involved in communication. The model he gives is supposed to be general enough to cover communication conducted by wire, direct speech, writing, or 'any other method'.

Hartley starts his considerations with some general remarks. E.g., he first formulates an abstract notion of a communication system. The elements of such a communication system are the following:

(A) A *set of physical symbols*, such as words, dots or dashes, and the like, which are correlated with meanings by convention. Such a system may, for example, consist of the words 'guitar', 'pepperoni', and 'screen' as three types of physical word tokens and will be related by convention with their respective meanings:

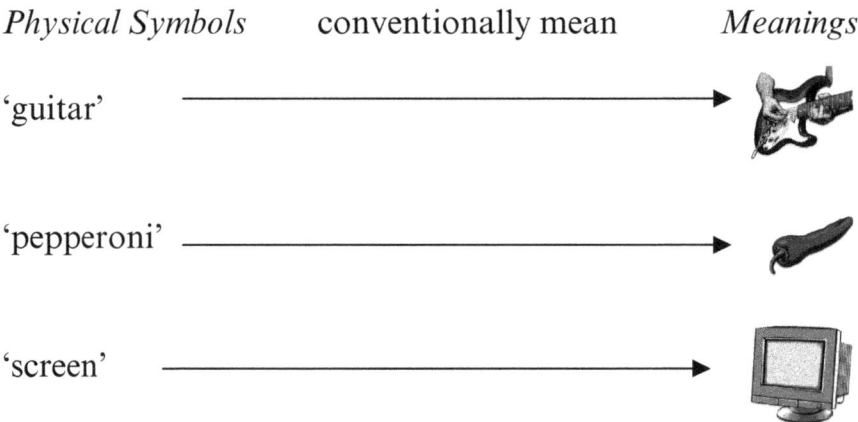

(B) A *sender*, who 'mentally' selects one of the physical symbols and uses his body to direct the attention of the receiver to the symbol selected. Such bodily motion might be the raising of his voice by using his vocal mechanism:

1. Sender *selects* a physical symbol:

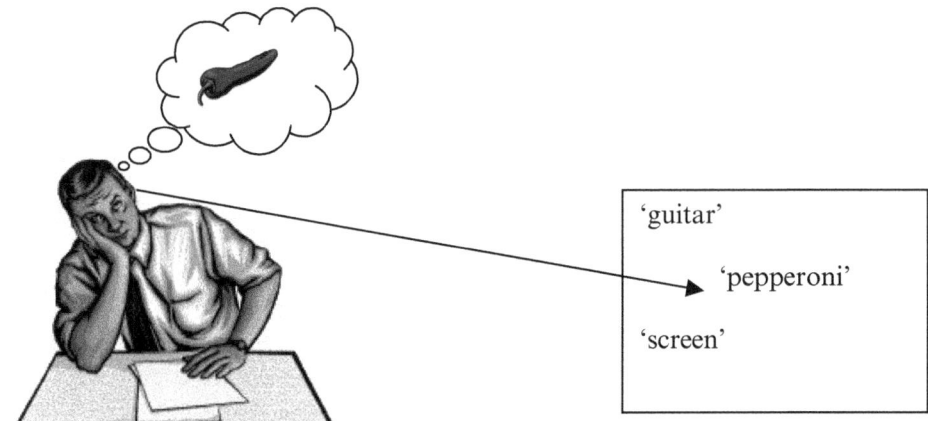

2. Sender directs the attention of the receiver to the symbol

(C) A receiver who has to reidentify the symbol chosen by the sender. The receiver's attention will be directed to something by the actions of

the sender, but the receiver has to identify the object of his attention as a sequence of physical symbols and as the very same sequence of physical symbols the sender has originally sent.

It was already clear to Hartley that this is the crucial step in transmitting information: the capacity of the communication system (A)-(C) will depend upon 'the possibility of distinguishing at the receiving end between the results of the various selections made at the sending end.' (Hartley 1928, 537). But let's have a closer look how information is produced at the sending end by making selections among symbols.

The Inverse Relationship of Information and Possibilities

Each time the sender chooses one of the symbols, he eliminates all other symbols which might have been chosen instead. Consider the letter that was sent to John Nyquist's father, Lars Johnsson. If there had been no address at all on the envelope, no symbols would have been chosen by the sender and thus no information conveyed as to whom the letter is intended to be sent. There are billions of possible addressees; no clue who the one is this letter belongs to.

Now consider that the sender had chosen the word 'Sweden' and had written it on the letter to direct the attention of the mailman to this symbol. That would have reduced the number of possible addressees quite a bit. Now the mailman knows that the addressee lives in Sweden. The number of possibilities is thus reduced from 6 billions (the number of people living on the planet) to approximately 8.8 millions (the number of people living in Sweden). Imagine that the sender also selects the symbol 'Värmland' and the symbol 'Johnsson' and the symbol 'Lars' and writes it on the envelope. Each selection reduces the number of possibilities again. The last symbol reduces the number of possibilities to two. The information on the envelope is, as we know, still not precise enough for the mailman to know who the addressee is. If the sender also selects the symbol 'Där Sör' and writes it on the envelope, the information is precise. It seems that the more possibilities are excluded by the selections made by the sender, the more information is produced. This inverse relationship between information and possibilities will accompany us throughout the whole book. This idea is clearly already part of Hartley's paper:

> By successive selections a sequence of symbols is brought to the listener's attention. At each selection there are eliminated all of the other symbols which might have been chosen. As the selection proceeds more and more possible symbol sequences are eliminated, and we say that the information becomes more precice. (Hartley 1928, 536)

It is not fully clear who first noted that there is such an inverse relationship between information and possibilities (here, possible selections of symbols). When we turn to the theory of semantic information as developed by Yehoshua Bar-Hillel and Rudolph Carnap in the next chapter, we will learn that at the heart of their theory is also such an inverse relationship principle. Carnap and Bar-Hillel motivate it by referring to the 'old philosophical principle *omnis determinatio est negatio*'. But this trace leads back to Hegel and his 'Science of Logic' (Hegel 1832, 101). Hegel himself claims to have the principle from Spinoza, who indeed wrote a similar sentence ('determinatio negatio est' in Spinoza 1674, 240). Neither in Spinoza, nor in Hegel it is terribly clear what this principle is supposed to mean. What is clear, though, is that both were neither concerned with information nor informational content nor with the preciseness of information, nor with possibilities and their exclusion. Thus it might be the case that Hartley is even among the first to formulate such an inverse relationship principle for information.

The 'Physical' and the 'Psychological' Aspects of Information

Nevertheless, the most interesting idea in Hartley's paper for the present chapter is certainly the plan to establish a measure of information 'in terms of purely physical quantities'. This is why this chapter is called 'The Syntactic Approach': linguistic meaning, and hence 'semantical' aspects of information are not considered by the approach developed by Nyquist, Hartley et al. Indeed, information as far as it might involve the interpretation of symbols by conscious agents is not of interest for the engineers at the Bell labs. 'Psychological factors' were to be eliminated in order to achieve a measure of information that could be applied to a communication system which is only physically specified. This measure was meant to be an objective feature of the communication system, independent of the knowledge and the skills of the person operating the system.

Consider a receiver identifies the following sequence of symbols from a telegraph:

(S)   .- .-. ... -.-. .... --. . ... .. -.-. .... -

In English (S) is a meaningless string of symbols, and a trained operator might notice that immediately. Not all sequences of symbols have assigned meaning and (S) is one of them. Therefore, if we count the possible symbol sequences out of which the sender chooses the message, the sequence above is not among the possible sequences if we take into account that the sender is an English speaker and that the sequence above is not a meaningful sequence in English.

However, in a different language (S) might very well be meaningful and thus might be among the possible sequences the sender is choosing from. Thus relative to a given language, different sets of symbol sequences turn out to be the possible sequences. Therefore, if a communication system consists of a set of possible symbols, a receiver and a sender, and the set of possible symbols varies from context to context, the system will be different for any given language. But then we are not describing an objective feature of the physical system.

This is why Hartley tries to 'eliminate' the psychological factors by ignoring the question of interpretation and regarding all symbol sequences as possible sequences. This leads him to distinguish primary and secondary symbols: Say the information transmitted via a telephone is a string of English words. The English words are the *secondary symbols* the message is made of. What the telephone transmits, though, is not a string of English words, but a sound wave which is the *primary symbol*. Secondary and primary symbols may stand in complicated relations. In a uniform code, each primary symbol coding a secondary symbol is of the same length as every other primary symbol. In non-uniform code this does not have to be the case (as in certain codes for telegraphy). Thus a uniform code might code all letters of the alphabet by a string of primary symbols (dots and dashes) which is of equal length (3 primary symbols) for every letter among the secondary symbols. On the other hand, might a non-uniform code represent the more frequently used letters (like 'e') with – say – only one primary symbol, and the less frequently used letters, like 'x', with more symbols.

In addition, the amount of information a signal contributes to the total information of a sequence of signals does – more often than not – progressively decrease. This is the case because due to, e.g., grammatical and semantical constraints not all sequences of symbols are possible. The sequence

Procrastination drinks bells

or

Green ideas sleep furiously

are impossible sequences, although each symbol (word) is among the possible symbols.

Therefore the amount of information contributed by a secondary symbol is again language dependent. To avoid these complications, Hartley chooses to measure the amount of information H transmitted by a sequence of symbols of length n as the logarithm of the number of possible symbol sequences s^n, whereby s is the number of primary symbols possible:

$$H = \log s^n$$
$$= n \log s$$

This is adequate only if all symbols chosen by the source are statistically independent. Hartley was thinking of a chance mechanism producing the information, in order to avoid any dependence on non-physical elements in his theory.

We will not go much deeper into Hartley's theory here. Most of his discoveries will return in a more precise form in the next chapter anyway. What we wanted to direct your attention to were the following aspects of Hartley's account:

 Hartley concentrated on the mere physical aspects of communication, leaving aside what he thought to be 'psychological'.

 He considered information to result from a selection among a certain set of possible symbols. The more selections are made, the more possibilities are excluded, the more precise is the resulting information.

The quantity of information *H* carried by a signal of n symbols in a code of s symbols is in his theory defined as *n log s*.

Neither in Hartley's nor in Nyquist's paper it is terribly clear why they define their measures of information (Hartley) or the speed at which 'intelligence' can be transmitted over a telegraph (Nyquist) as a log function. Nyquist's motivation seems to be a mere technical point:

> There is a difference, which is not of great significance from the standpoint of pure theory, but which is important from the standpoint of practical computation. [...] In fact, by expressing the characteristic in terms of a logarithmic function [...] it is possible to reduce these operations to additions. (Nyquist 1924, 627)

As we will see in the next chapter, there is even a motivation from pure theory to state information theory in terms of a logarithmic function.

Further Reading
For some background in thermodynamics and the story of Maxwell's demon we suggest

   Harvey S. Leff/Andrew F. Rex (eds.), *Maxwell's Demon. Entropy, Information, Computing*, Adam Hilger 1990.

This is a well introduced collection of all important physics papers dealing with Maxwell's demon. For students who are less interested in the physical details, but still want to know more about the history of thermodynamics and Maxwell's demon in particular, we suggest the popular scientific book

   Hans Christian von Baeyer, *Warmth Disperses and Time Passes. The History of Heat*. New York 1999.

For more on the historical background of Communication Theory not covered here, see

- E. Colin Cherry, 'The Communication of Information (A Historical Review)', *The American Scientist* 40, 640-664.

and

- John R. Pierce, *An Introduction to Information Theory*. Symbols, Signals and Noise, New York 1980.

1|2 The Syntactic Approach to Information II

Claude E. Shannon

The hero of this chapter is Claude Elwood Shannon, the son of another Claude Elwood Shannon and Mabel Catherine Wolf. Claude was born in Petoskey, Michigan, on April 30, 1916. He graduated from the University of Michigan in 1936 with bachelor's degrees in mathematics and electrical engineering. In 1940 he earned both a master's degree in electrical engineering and a Ph.D. in mathematics from the Massachusetts Institute of Technology (MIT).

Shannon had an impressively broad range of interests. He wrote his MA thesis, *A Symbolic Analysis of Relay and Switching Circuit,* on the theoretical underpinnings of digital circuits, using Boolean Algebra. This work is one of the milestones for modern computer technology, it was here that Shannon discovered the similarity between Boolean Algebra and telephone switching circuits. Nevertheless, the work he is most famous for is his 1948 paper 'The Mathematical Theory of Communication' which appeared in the *Bell System Technical Journal.*

Mathematical Communication Theory

At the beginning of Shannon's theory of information lies the observation, which was made already by Hartley, that 'the fundamental problem of communication is that of reproducing at one point either exactly or approximately a message selected at another point' (Shannon 1948, 5). The two following sentences of Shannon's 1948 paper also state fundamental points arrived at by Hartley and Nyquist already. One is that the 'semantic aspects of communication are irrelevant to the engineering problem', the other is that the communication system will be considered to be a device which at one end chooses from a set of possible messages and must be designed to operate for each possible message.

The communication model of Shannon is more sophisticated than the one considered by Hartley. Its components are an information source, a transmitter, a communication channel, a noise source, a receiver, and a destination. Hartley's 'symbol' is here analyzed into a

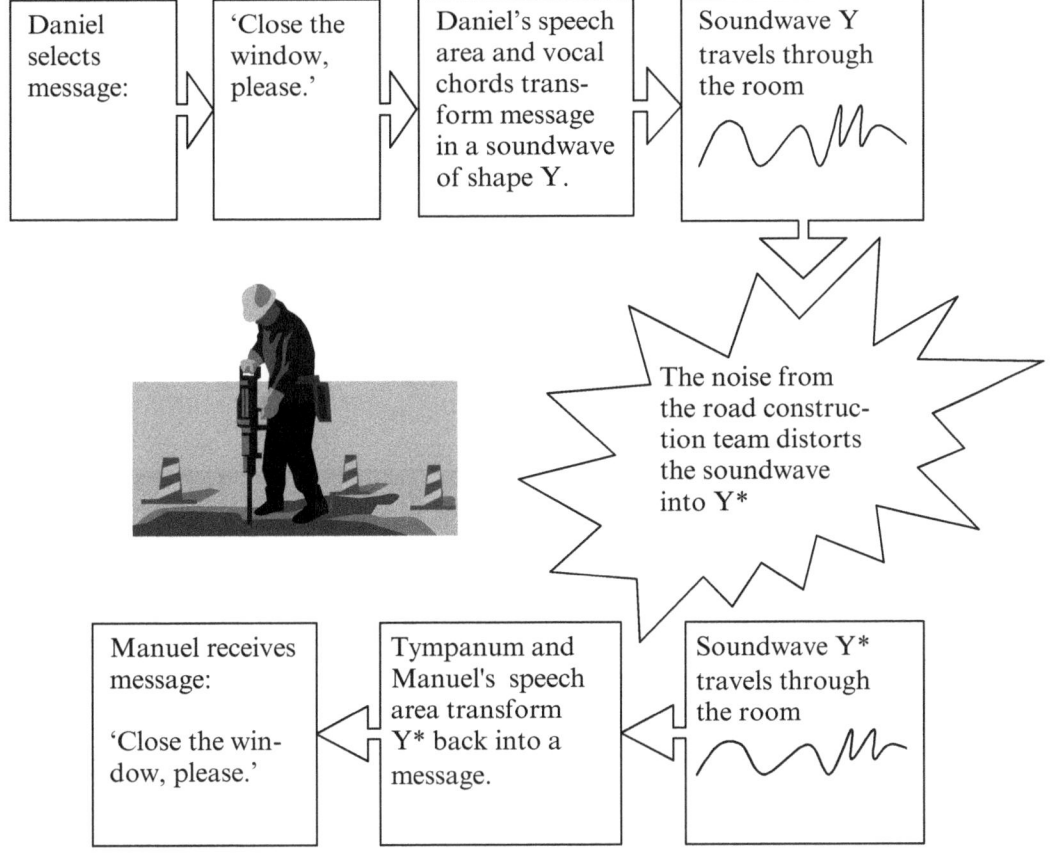

Figure 1|2–1

sent message, a signal, a received signal and a received message. Let's see how these components work together.

Consider the situation as depicted in figure 1|2–1: I'm freezing and want Manuel to close the window. I select a message for Manuel: 'Close the window, please.' The speech area of my brain together with my vocal cords produce a soundwave of shape Y. The soundwave moves through the room towards Manuel. Outside the room is a road construction team at work. It is noisy in the room and the soundwave that travels towards Manuel gets distorted from Y to Y*. Y* eventually hits Manuel's ear. His tympanum and his brain convert Y* back into a message in Manuel's language of mind: 'Close the window, please.' Fortunately the distortion of the soundwave was not too se-

THE SYNTACTIC APPROACH TO INFORMATION II

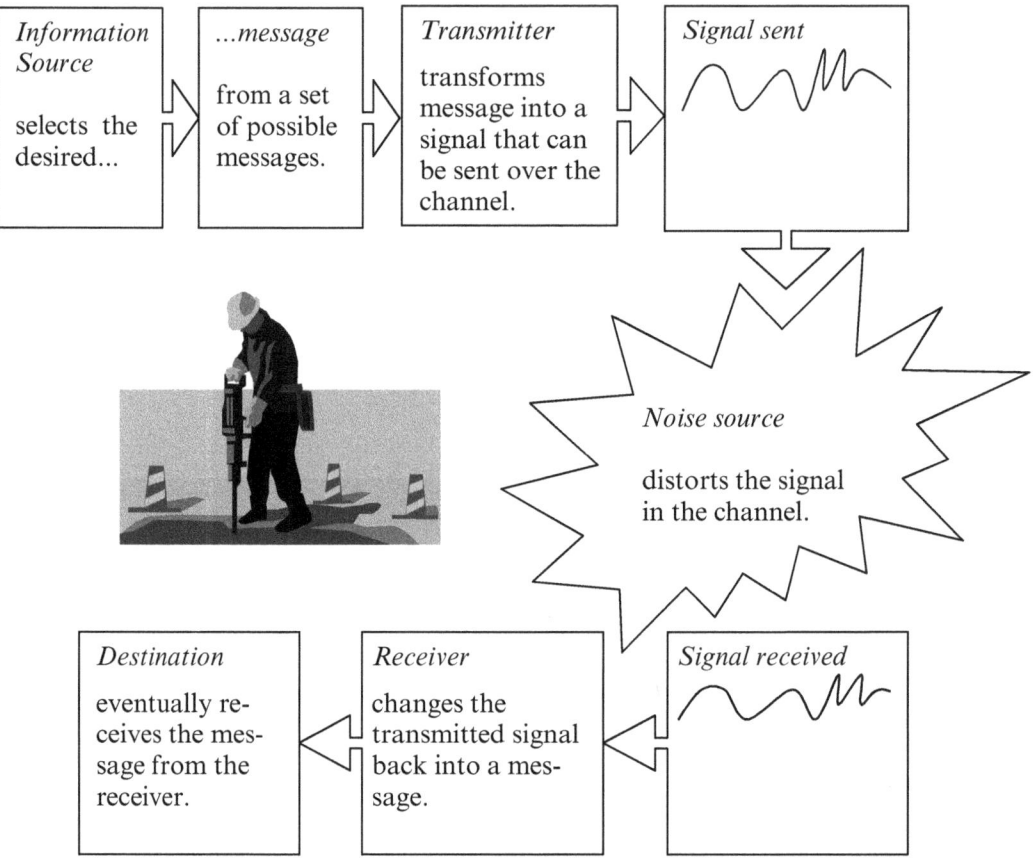

Figure 1|2–2

vere for Manuel to understand my message. He closes the window. Figure 1|2–2 gives a schematic representation of the communication situation described in our little story. It identifies the components of a communication system according to Shannon.

Shannon developed a mathematical theory to investigate and to describe what goes on when information is transmitted via such a communication system. The following questions are addressed by Shannon's account:

1. How does one measure *amount* of information?

2. How does one measure the *capacity* of an information channel independent of the other factors?

3. Transmitting a message into a signal and back involves a *coding* process. When is such a process efficient?

4. What is *noise*? How can noise be measured and how can its undesirable effects be eliminated?

5. What is the difference between a *continuous* and a *discrete* symbol?

For now, we will only highlight the main characteristics of his theory that you will need to understand the significance of MCT for the development of semantical information theory. We will thus start with the most important aspect of Shannon's theory for our purposes: what is information and how can it be measured?

Information

As we have noted quite often already, information is a term with a broad meaning. *Mathematical Communication Theory* (MCT) is not a theory that was developed to cover all aspects of 'information' as it is used in common language and pre-scientific talk. MCT was developed to deal with certain engineering problems. It was of interest for the engineers at Bell to measure and improve the transmission rate of communication devices such as telephones, telegraphs or TV sets. What was called for was a technical concept of information that could serve this purpose, that could be used to measure the capacities of physically described communication systems.

Therefore the first requirement the concept of information had to meet was that information is quantitative: a message might be more or less informative, a symbol might carry more or less information, a channel might allow to transmit more or less information per units of time. But how can information be measured? As we suggested already in the last chapter, there seems to be a certain inverse relationship between information and uncertainty.

Consider for example an information source that always produces the same signal and is known to produce always the same signal. Such a source produces zero information. Imagine a red light that is mounted to an engine. Say it is lit if the temperature of the engine is equal or above 50°C and is also lit if the temperature is anywhere below 50°C. If we don't know anything else about the red light and receive the 'information' that it is lit, this doesn't tell us anything. Of course it is lit, it always is. Such a source cannot produce any information.

Now, consider a system which is slightly more complex than our red light. Consider a binary device like a fair coin C, with its two equiprobable symbols $\{h, t\}$. If we are the receiver, know the source, and wait for a symbol, we are uncertain as to which symbol the source will produce. We are in a state of *data deficit*, the 'uncertainty' in Shannon's terms. Once we receive a symbol, say 'h', our *uncertainty decreases*, and we remark that we have received some *information*. That is the inverse relationship between information and uncertainty. Now, how can information be measured? Since the likelihood of events is involved, we will have to turn to probability theory.

We shall call a *complete system* of events $A_1, A_2, ..., A_n$ a system of events which is such that exactly one of the events must occur at each trial. As in the case of our fair coin C, either h or t and only one of them must occur after each time throwing the coin. In the case of C, where the number of possible events (n) is 2, we have a simple alternative pair of mutually exclusive events. In this case we have a *finite scheme*, we are given the possible events $\{h, t\}$ and – because we know that it is a fair coin – know their respective probabilities ($p(h) = p(t) = .5$), which – since these are all the events to occur (it is a *complete* system) – add up to one:

> **Definition 1|2–1 (Finite Scheme)**
>
> If we are given the events $A_1, A_2, ..., A_n$ of a complete system, together with their probabilities $p_1, p_2, ..., p_n$ ($p_i \geq 0$, $\sum_{i=1}^{n} p_i = 1$), then we say that we have a *finite scheme*
>
> $$A = \begin{pmatrix} A_1 \; A_2 \; ... \; A_n \\ p_1 \; p_2 \; ... \; p_n \end{pmatrix}$$

If we consider a 'true' die instead of a fair coin, and designate the appearance of a certain number (i) of points by A_i ($1 \leq i \leq 6$), then we have the following finite scheme:

$$A = \begin{pmatrix} A_1 & A_2 & A_3 & A_4 & A_5 & A_6 \\ \dfrac{1}{6} & \dfrac{1}{6} & \dfrac{1}{6} & \dfrac{1}{6} & \dfrac{1}{6} & \dfrac{1}{6} \end{pmatrix}$$

As we have said already, when we learn which number of points the die shows, our uncertainty is reduced, the uncertainty, which is described by such a finite scheme.

In the case of the die, as in the case of the fair coin, we have sofar only considered events with equal probabilities. That is $p(A_1) = p(A_2) = ... p(A_n)$. Compare the following experiments E_1 and E_2, the outcomes of which are described by the two finite schemes:

(E_1) $\begin{pmatrix} A_1 & A_2 \\ .5 & .5 \end{pmatrix}$

(E_2) $\begin{pmatrix} A_1 & A_2 \\ .99 & .01 \end{pmatrix}$

In the first case both outcomes are equally likely, in the second case, however, the outcome A_2 is highly unlikely to occur. We would certainly not expect A_2 to occur. It seems that in the second case the uncertainty, which of the possible results is going to be the outcome of the experiment, should be different from the uncertainty in the first case, in particular the uncertainty should be less.

But the difference in uncertainty seems to have influence on the amount of information generated. If we learn in E_2, that A_1 has occured, this is not that informative, for given the high probability of this event, we have expected it anyway.

In contrast, learning that in E_1, A_1 has occured is more informative, A_1 and A_2 in E_1 were equally likely to occur and we thus had no clue which of them would be the outcome of the experiment. Therefore, *on average*, in E_2 it is likely to get a not very informative result, whereas in E_1 you will get a quite informative result in any case.

Shannon introduced the following formula to measure the amount of uncertainty associated with a given finite sheme. We will call this the *entropy of a finite sheme*.

Definition 1|2–2 (Entropy of a Finite Scheme)

For a givene finite sheme A:

$$A = \begin{pmatrix} A_1 \; A_2 \; ... \; A_n \\ p_1 \; p_2 \; ... \; p_n \end{pmatrix}$$

We shall call

$$H(p_1, p_2, ..., p_n) = -\sum_{k=1}^{n} p_k \log p_k$$

the *entropy of A*, taking the logarithms to an arbitrary but fixed base and $p_k \log p_k = 0$ if $p_k = 0$.

Why this formula can serve as a measure of uncertainty will be shown in a minute. But for the mathematically innocent reader we will briefly say some things about the use of log-functions that we have already introduced in the preceeding chapter (following the exposition in Schneider 2000). If you feel familiar with log functions you might want to skip the next section.

Understanding Logarithms

As we had seen in the previous chapter, log functions were already used by Nyquist and Hartley for technical reasons. Nyquist found it easier to do the computations with log expressions, but he did not think there was a theoretical reason to choose log functions. Here we can now add a theoretical reason, although it is a rather soft one. Multiplication turns into Addition when converted into log functions. That is rather unimportant from a mathematical point of view, but of interest when we try to construct a theory that meshes with our pre-theoretic intuitions. We want information to be additive when we consider the information that is produced by two independent events. Log functions allow us to preserve this intuition in the calculations of our theory.

We assume that you are familiar with the mathematical operation of addition and multiplication. You might also know that exponentiation is the extension of multiplication (as multiplication can be considered the extension of addition):

$$2 \times 2 \times 2 = 2^3 = 8$$

This is read 'two raised to the third is eight'. Because exponentiation counts the number of multiplications, the exponents add:

$$2^2 \times 2^3 = 2^{2+3} = 2^5$$

The number '2' is called the base of the exponentiation. If we raise the exponent to another exponent, the values multiply:

$$(2^2)^3 = 2^2 \times 2^2 \times 2^2 = 2^{2+2+2} = 2^{2 \times 3} = 2^6$$

Now, consider that we have a number and we want to know how many 2's must be multiplied together to get 32? That is, we want to solve this equation:

$$2^B = 32$$

Of course, $2^5 = 32$, so $B = 5$. This function is called the logarithm:

$$\log_2 32 = 5$$

We read this as 'the logarithm to the base 2 of 32 is 5'. It is the 'inverse function' for exponentiation.

$$2^{\log_2 a} = a \text{ and } \log_2(2^a) = a$$

Now, consider this equation:

$$2^{a+b} = 2^a \times 2^b$$

Take the logarithm of both sides:

$$\log_2 2^{a+b} = \log_2 (2^a \times 2^b)$$

Since exponentiation and the logarithm are inverse operations, we can collapse the left side:

$$a + b = \log_2 (2^a \times 2^b)$$

Now we substitute: $\log_2 x = a$ and $\log_2 y = b$:

$$\log_2 x + \log_2 y = \log_2(2^{\log_2 x} \times 2^{\log_2 y})$$

Again, exponentiation and the logarithm are inverse operations, so we can collapse the two cases on the right side:

$$\log_2 x + \log_2 y = \log_2 (x \times y)$$

This is the additive property that allows us to turn multiplications into additions when we convert all values into their logarithms. To use the base 2 instead of any other base (e.g., the common or 'Briggs' logarithm to the base 10) is not fully arbitrary either. It allows us to measure information in bits, binary *units* of information, which meshes nicely with the fact that we often use binary *digits* to encode information nowadays (do not confuse these two notions of 'bits' we will explain their difference later in this chapter).

Properties of Entropy

Now we will return to the entropy of a finite scheme as defined in Definition 1|2–2. What are the properties of this function that make it a reasonable measure of entropy?

You might have noticed already that $H(p_1, p_2,..., p_n) = 0$ iff one of the probabilities in the finite scheme is 1 (and all the others zero). In this case we have a finite scheme that in fact consists of only one possible event. If the finite scheme describes the uncertainty of an experiment, we could predict with complete certainty the outcome of the experiment. But if there is no uncertainty that could be reduced by the experiment, there is no information gained by conducting it. In all other cases, however, the entropy of a finite scheme is positive.

Moreover, for a fixed number of possible events *n*, the scheme with the highest uncertainty should be the one with equally likely outcomes. Remember our experiments E_1 and E_2 from above, the uncertainty associated with E_1 was higher than the one intuitively associated with E_2. In E_2 we would predict A_1 being the outcome of the experiment, whereas in the case of E_1 we would refrain from making any predictions. Now, what about *H*? Does the defined function for the entropy of a finite scheme assume its largest value for equally likely outcomes? (The answer is yes, and you might skip the following paragraph on a first reading).

Proof 1

To prove this we first have to consider what it means to have equally likely outcomes in a finite scheme. Obviously, this means that $p_k = 1/n$ ($k = 1, 2, ...,n$). For the proof we may use the following inequality which is valid for any continuous convex function $\varphi(x)$:

$$\varphi\left(\frac{1}{n}\sum_{k=1}^{n}a_k\right) \leq \frac{1}{n}\sum_{k=1}^{n}\varphi(a_k)$$

where $a_1, a_2, ..., a_n$ are any positive numbers. To apply this inequality to our case, we will set $a_k = p_k$ and $\varphi(x) = x \log x$. Since finite schemes are complete, we know that $\sum_{k=1}^{n} p_k = 1$. Therefore we find

$$\varphi\left(\frac{1}{n}\right) = \frac{1}{n}\log\frac{1}{n} \leq \frac{1}{n}\sum_{k=1}^{n} p_k \log p_k = -\frac{1}{n}H(p_1, p_2, ..., p_n)$$

whence

$$H(p_1, p_2, ..., p_n) \leq \log n = H\left(\frac{1}{n}, \frac{1}{n}, ..., \frac{1}{n}\right) \square$$

(By the way, we will use '$\square$' instead of 'Q.E.D' to mark the end of a proof.)

Additivity of Independent and Dependent Schemes

So far we have only considered an isolated finite scheme. But consider that instead of only learning what the outcome of one experiment was, say E_1, you got to know the outcome of another experiment, say E_2, too. If the two experiments are independent of each other, i.e. what is happening in E_1 does not influence what happens at E_2 and vice versa, the information about the outcome of the two events should be the sum of the information you had obtained from only a single event. Likewise, the uncertainty of both experiments taken together should be the sum of the uncertainties associated with each single experiment. What about H in such cases?

Consider two finite schemes:

$$A = \begin{pmatrix} A_1 \, A_2 \ldots A_n \\ p_1 \, p_2 \cdots p_n \end{pmatrix}, \quad B = \begin{pmatrix} B_1 \, B_2 \ldots B_n \\ q_1 \, q_2 \cdots q_n \end{pmatrix}$$

and let them both be mutually independent, i.e., the probability π_{kl} of the joint occurrence of the events A_k and B_l is the product $p_k q_l$. The set of joint occurrences of events now forms another finite scheme, viz. the set of events $A_k B_l$ ($1 \leq k \leq n$, $1 \leq l \leq m$), with probabilities π_{kl}, which we call the *product* of A and B, AB.

Let $H(A)$, $H(B)$, and $H(AB)$ be the entropies of the finite schemes A, B, and AB, then we find in fact that H is additive in the way considered above:

$$H(AB) = H(A) + H(B)$$

This can easily be seen from the fact that

$$-H(AB) = \sum_k \sum_l \pi_{kl} \log \pi_{kl} = \sum_k \sum_l p_k q_l (\log p_k + q_l) =$$

$$= \sum_k p_k \log p_k \sum_l q_l + \sum_l q_l \log q_l \sum_k p_k = -H(A) - H(B) \; \square$$

So additivity is given, if we consider two independent events, or two independent sources. But what happens if two events are statistically dependent? Consider a source that produces only meaningful English sentences, we call it 'Paula'. The set of English words is large, but fortunately finite. Each word of the English language might – given an appropriately chosen situation – have a particular probability to be the first word uttered by our source. Some words are more frequently used than others, especially given the fact that the word has the first position in a new utterance.

Let us assume that the probability for the event that Paula utters 'Hi' as the first word in a new utterance is p and the probability that she utters 'Fish' as the first word in a new utterance is q. Given the appropriate circumstances $p > q$. Now she utters 'Hi':
Does this influence the probabilities for the second word in this utter-

ance? Well, presumably it does. Consider how likely it is that Paula is going to say 'Hi, how are you?' and how comparatively unlikely it is that she is going to utter 'Hi, off ...'. If you meet Paula in an appropriate situation you therefore might expect her to say 'how' as the next word, rather than 'off', after she has uttered 'hi' already. Had Paula uttered some other word as the first word of the utterance, e.g. 'Keep', the probabilities for 'off' and 'how' would be qualitatively different. In this case the probability for 'off' would be higher. Therefore the informativeness of 'hi, how' cannot simply be the sum of the informativeness of 'hi' from the finite scheme FIRST WORD OF THE UTTERANCE and of 'how' from the finite scheme SECOND WORD OF THE UTTERANCE. The schemes FIRST WORD OF THE UTTERANCE and SECOND WORD OF THE UTTERANCE are not independent.

We denote q_{kl} the probability that the event B_l of the scheme B occurs, given that the event A_k of the scheme A occured, such that

$$\pi_{kl} = p_k q_{kl} \ (1 \leq k \leq n, 1 \leq l \leq m).$$

Then

$$-H(AB) = \sum_k \sum_l p_k q_{kl} (\log p_k + \log q_{kl}) =$$

$$= \sum_k p_k \log p_k \sum_l q_{kl} + \sum_k p_k \sum_l q_{kl} \log q_{kl}$$

For any k, $\sum_l q_{kl} = 1$; and the conditional entropy $H_k(B)$ of the scheme B, calculated on the assumption that the event A_k of the scheme A occured, is given by the sum $-\sum_l q_{kl} \log q_{kl}$.

With this, we obtain

$$H(AB) = H(A) + \sum_k p_k H_k(B)$$

$H_k(B)$ being a random variable in the scheme A. The value of $H_k(B)$ is completely determined by which event A_k of the scheme A actually occured. So we can consider the last term of the right side as the mathematical expectation of the quantity $H(B)$ in the scheme A and designate this by $H_A(B)$. For the most general case, we obtain

$$H(AB) = H(A) + H_A(B).$$

If A and B are independent, the relation reduces to $H(AB) = H(A) + H(B)$.

This relation has the nice property that in all cases $H_A(B) \leq H(B)$. What does this mean? Well, having received information, for example information about which event A_k of the scheme A actually occurred, should at best reduce your uncertainty about which event of the scheme B will now occur, but it certainly should not raise that uncertainty above the uncertainty of the scheme B alone. Information about an event should not make you more ignorant than you were before. This is easily proven, but you might again skip the next paragraph on a first reading.

Proof 2

We begin again with the observation that every continuous convex function $f(x)$ obeys the following inequality

$$\sum_k \lambda_k f(x_k) \geq f\left(\sum_k \lambda_k x_k\right)$$

if $\lambda_k \geq 0$ and $\sum_k \lambda_k = 1$. Now we again set $f(x) = x \log x$, $\lambda_k = p_k$, $x_k = q_{kl}$. We then find for arbitrary l:

$$\sum_k p_k q_{kl} \log q_{kl} \geq \left(\sum_k p_k q_{kl}\right) \log\left(\sum_k p_k q_{kl}\right) = q_l \log q_l$$

since $\sum_k p_k q_{kl} = q_l$. We can now sum over l, thereby obtaining on the left side of this inequality the quantity

$$\sum_k p_k \sum_l q_{kl} \log q_{kl} = -\sum_k p_k H_k(B) = -H_A(B)$$

and finally arrive at

$$-H_A(B) \geq \sum_l q_l \log q_l = -H(B) \quad \square$$

Taking a Breath

We have now inspected some of the properties of entropy that make it a reasonable measure of information. To summarize, we found the following:

 The information produced by the source consists in removing the uncertainty which existed before the source made the selection of the message.

 The larger this uncertainty, the larger we consider to be the amount of information obtained by removing it.

The uncertainty associated with a finite scheme A is $H(A)$, the *entropy* of A.

 Consider two finite schemes A and B and their product AB. If the two schemes are independent, the information given by the realization of AB is the sum of the realization of the schemes A and B. $H(AB) = H(A) + H(B)$

 The amount of information given by the realization of two finite schemes A and B equals the amount of information given by the realization of scheme A, plus the mathematical expectation of the amount of additional information by the realization of scheme B after the realization of scheme A.

 The amount of information given by the realization of a scheme B can only decrease if another scheme A is realized beforehand.

The Uniqueness Theorem for Entropy

The entropy expression that we have introduced above and for which we have now discussed some of its interesting properties, is not merely some arbitrary function that has these properties, but actually the *unique* function that has such properties. This is a very interesting result and we will give the proof her (following the proof given by A. I. Khinchin, who also proved the propositions that we have considered so far).

We have already convinced ourselves of the fact that the following two properties are properties we would intuitively expect from an information measure:

1. For given n and for $\sum_{k=1}^{n} p_k = 1$, the function $H(p_1, p_2, ..., p_n)$ takes its largest value for $p_k = 1/n$ ($k = 1, 2, ..., n$).

2. $H(AB) = H(A) + H_A(B)$

This much is already familiar. We shall now add a third property which seems reasonable to expect from our definition of entropy. Consider the following two finite schemes A and B:

$$A = \begin{pmatrix} A_1 \; A_2 \; ... \; A_n \\ p_1 \; p_2 \; ... \; p_n \end{pmatrix}, \quad B = \begin{pmatrix} A_1 \; A_2 \; ... \; A_n \; A_{n+1} \\ p_1 \; p_2 \; ... \; p_n \quad 0 \end{pmatrix}$$

The only difference between A and B is that B also contains the impossible event. It seems quite reasonable to assume the entropies $H(A)$ and $H(B)$ to be the same, since the difference between A and B is certainly not substantial. Therefore

3. $H(p_1, p_2, ..., p_n, 0) = H(p_1, p_2, ..., p_n)$. (Adding any number of impossible events to a scheme does not change its entropy.)

Now we are sufficiently equipped to prove the following theorem:

> **Theorem 1|2–1 (Uniqueness Theorem)**
>
> Let $H(p_1, p_2, ..., p_n)$ be a function defined for any integer n and for all values $p_1, p_2, ..., p_n$ such that $p_k \geq 0$ ($k = 1, 2, ..., n$), $\sum_{k=1}^{n} p_k = 1$. If for any n this function is continuous with respect to all its arguments, and if it has the properties 1, 2, and 3, then
>
> $$H(p_1, p_2, ..., p_n) = -\lambda \sum_{k=1}^{n} p_k \log p_k$$
>
> where λ is a positive constant.

Proof 3

Since this might again be mathematically complicated (and is rather lengthy) you might want to jump on to the next paragraph on a first reading.

As an abbreviation we set

$$H\left(\frac{1}{n},\frac{1}{n},...,\frac{1}{n}\right) = L(n)$$

we shall show that $L(n) = \lambda \log n$, where λ is a positive constant. By properties 3 (impossible event) and 1 (highest entropy), we have

$$L(n) = H\left(\frac{1}{n},\frac{1}{n},...,\frac{1}{n},0\right) \leq H\left(\frac{1}{n+1},\frac{1}{n+1},...,\frac{1}{n+1}\right) = L(n+1)$$

so that $L(n)$ is a non-decreasing function of n. Consider m mutually independent finite schemes $S_1, S_2, ..., S_m$ each of which contains r equally likely events (m and r being positive integers):

$$H(S_k) = H\left(\frac{1}{r},\frac{1}{r},...,\frac{1}{r}\right) = L(r) \quad (1 \leq k \leq m)$$

If we generalize property 2 (additivity) to the case of m schemes, we have – since all schemes S_k are mutually independent –

$$H(S_1 S_2 ... S_m) = \sum_{k=1}^{m} H(S_k) = mL(r)$$

The product scheme out of all S_1 to S_m, $S_1 S_2 ... S_m$, obviously consists of r^m equally likely events, so that the entropy is $L(r^m)$. Therefore we now have

(4) $\quad L(r^m) = mL(r)$

and also for any other pair of positive integers n and s

(5) $\quad L(s^n) = nL(s)$.

We can choose the numbers r, s, and n arbitrarily but have the number m be determined by the following inequalities:

(6) $\quad r^m \leq s^n \leq r^{m+1}$

so we get

(7) $\quad m \log r \leq n \log s < (m+1) \log r,$

$$\frac{m}{n} \leq \frac{\log s}{\log r} < \frac{m}{n} + \frac{1}{n}$$

Given the inequalities that characterize m (6), it follows by the monotonicity of $L(n)$ that

$$L(r^m) \leq L(s^n) \leq L(r^{m+1})$$

and therefore, by (4) and (5)

$$mL(r) \leq nL(s) \leq (m+1)L(r),$$

such that

(8) $\quad \dfrac{m}{n} \leq \dfrac{L(s)}{L(r)} \leq \dfrac{m}{n} + \dfrac{1}{n}$

From (7) and (8) we get

$$\left| \frac{L(s)}{L(r)} - \frac{\log s}{\log r} \right| \leq \frac{1}{n}$$

Now the left side of this last inequality is independent of m, and since n can be chosen arbitrarily large in the right side, we get

$$\frac{L(s)}{\log s} = \frac{L(r)}{\log r}$$

since we have chosen r and s arbitrarily, this means that

$$L(n) = \lambda \log n$$

where λ is a constant. By the monotonicity of $L(n)$, we know $\lambda \geq 0$ and so we arrive at the result for the special case, $p_k = 1/n$ ($1 \leq k \leq n$).

We will now consider the more general case and the $p_k(1, 2, ..., n)$ are any rational numbers. Let

$$p_k = \frac{g_k}{g} \quad (k = 1, 2, ..., n)$$

where all g_k are positive integers and $\sum_{k=1}^{n} g_k = g$. Let the finite scheme A consist of n events with the probabilities $p_1, p_2, ..., p_n$. We now want to define the entropy for this scheme. To this end, we consider another scheme B, which is dependent on A and defined as follows: The scheme B contains g events $B_1, B_2, ..., B_g$, which we divide in n groups, containing $g_1, g_2, ..., g_n$ events, respectively. If the event A_k occurred in scheme A, then in scheme B all the g_k events of the k'th group have the same probability $1/g_k$, and all the events of the other groups have probability zero (are impossible events). Thus, given any outcome A_k of the scheme A, the scheme B reduces to a system g_k of equally likely events, so that the conditional entropy

$$H_k(B) = H\left(\frac{1}{g_k}, \frac{1}{g_k}, ... \frac{1}{g_k}\right) = L(g_k) = \lambda \log g_k$$

which means

(9) $\quad H_A(B) = \sum_{k=1}^{n} p_k H_k(B) = \lambda \sum_{k=1}^{n} p_k \log g_k = \lambda \sum_{k=1}^{n} p_k \log p_k + \lambda \log g.$

Let us now return to the product scheme AB, consisting of the events $A_k B_l$ ($1 \leq k \leq n$, $1 \leq l \leq g$). Such an event is among the possible events only if B_l belongs to the k'th group. Thus the number of possible events

$A_k B_l$ for a given k is g_k, and the total number of possible events in the scheme AB is $\sum_{k=1}^{n} g_k = g$. The probability of each possible event $A_k B_l$ is then $p_k/g_k = 1/g$, which is the same for all events. Thus the scheme AB consists of g equally likely events, and therefore

$$H(AB) = L(g) = \lambda \log g.$$

If we use property 2 again, as well as equation (9), we get

$$\lambda \log g = H(A) + \lambda \sum_{k=1}^{n} p_k \log p_k$$

hence

(10) $$H(A) = H(p_1, p_2, ..., p_n) = -\lambda \sum_{k=1}^{n} p_k \log p_k$$

Now, relation (10) which we proved for rational p_1, p_2, ..., p_n must be valid for any values of its arguments because of the continuity of $H(p_1, p_2, ..., p_n)$ that we postulated in the beginning. ❑

The Channel

Remembering our diagram from figure 1|2–2, you might wonder how much we have learned so far about a communication system. According to Shannon, such a system consists of an information source, a transmitter, a channel, a receiver, and a destination, as well as a message and a signal. Until now we have only talked about the information source and the message. What we have learned is how to calculate the amount of information that is produced at a source on average, given that it selects messages from a finite set of possible messages with definite probabilities. Now we will send our message on its way through the channel and observe what we can learn from MCT about this.

As we have said already, the selected message is first accepted by a *transmitter* and there turned into a *signal*. In our example this was done by the vocal chords that turned the signal into a soundwave. If the example had involved an additional telephone connection, this would have involved the transmission of the audible voice signal into a varying electrical current in the telephone wire (at least when using analog technology), if it had involved telegraphy, the transmitter would have had to code the message first into a sequence of dots and dashes. This signal is then sent through the communication channel, a telephone wire, a room, etc.

The capacity of channels was of special concern for the people working at the Bell labs. They were engineers and wanted to know what the technical limits of different channels are. Given the work done by Hartley and Shannon, this capacity can now be measured in terms of the amount of information a channel can transmit in a given unit of time rather than in terms of the number of symbols.

Consider a source (a finite scheme) and an appropriate transmitter-such that each signal corresponding to a possible message chosen represents s bits of information, the symbols being of the same duration and the channel being such that it can transmit n such symbols per second, the capacity C of the channel is defined to be $n \times s$ bits per second. In the general case one has also to account for the varying lengths of the possible symbols and has to take into account that not all possible sequences of symbols may be allowed). In this case the channel capacity is given by

$$C = \lim_{T \to \infty} \frac{\log N(T)}{T}$$

$N(T)$ being the number of allowed signals of duration T.

The Transmitter and Receiver: Coding

Given a channel with a certain capacity C and given an information source that produces a certain average amount of information H, information can flow at different speeds, if the coding is not done efficiently.

Consider the product of a finite scheme AB. We can consider AB to be a system of two coins thrown, A and B are hence independent. Each symbol of the possible symbols of AB occurs with probability .25.

$$AB = \begin{pmatrix} \langle h,h \rangle \langle h,t \rangle \langle t,h \rangle \langle t,t \rangle \\ .25 \quad .25 \quad .25 \quad .25 \end{pmatrix}$$

Now imagine that we want to code the results produced at AB.

A simple way of encoding its symbols is to associate each of them with two digits:

Code$_1$

events		code
$\langle h, h \rangle$	=	'00'
$\langle h, t \rangle$	=	'01'
$\langle t, h \rangle$	=	'10'
$\langle t, t \rangle$	=	'11'

In this Code$_1$ a message conveys 2 bits of information, as expected. We must not confuse *bits* as *bi*-nary uni*ts* of information (recall that we decided to use $\log_2$ only as a matter of convenience) with *bits* as *bi*-nary digi*ts*, which is what a 2-symbols system uses to encode a message.

Suppose that a variant, the AB^* system, is biased, and that the four symbols occur with the following probabilities:

$$AB^* = \begin{pmatrix} \langle h,h \rangle \langle h,t \rangle \langle t,h \rangle \langle t,t \rangle \\ .5 \quad .25 \quad .125 \quad .125 \end{pmatrix}$$

If we calculate $H(AB)$, chosing 2 as the base for log (as we will do from now on), we find that the entropy is 2 bits (binary units of information) per symbol. Using a two bit (binary digits) code, as we did above in Code$_1$, is thus an efficient way of coding AB, for two bits of information we use two binary digits. We know, however, that H has its maximum in the case of equiprobable events, thus $H(AB) > H(AB^*)$, so by using $Code_1$ we would be wasting resources in the case of $H(AB^*)$.

A more efficient $Code_2$ should take into account the symbols' probabilities, with the following outcomes:

$Code_2$

$\langle h, h \rangle =$	'0'	$.5 \times 1$	binary digit	$= .5$
$\langle h, t \rangle =$	'10'	$.25 \times 2$	binary digits	$= .5$
$\langle t, h \rangle =$	'110'	$.125 \times 3$	binary digits	$= .375$
$\langle t, t \rangle =$	'111'	$.125 \times 3$	binary digits	$= .375$

In $Code_2$, known as Fano Code, a message conveys 1.75 bits of information. How does one arrive at such a code? Consider the following example (from Pierce 1961): Suppose the symbols we start with are the eight words 'the', 'man', 'to', 'runs', 'house', 'likes', 'horse', 'sells'. We shall assume that these words occurr independently with the probabilities of appearance as given in figure 1|2–3.

If we compute the entropy per word, using the entropy formula from above (and take 2 as the base), we arrive at an entropy of 2.21 bits per word. Therefore, using 3 binary digits to code for each of the eight

Word	Probability
the	.05
man	.15
to	.12
runs	.10
house	.04
likes	.04
horse	.03
sells	.02

Figure 1|2–3

words ($2^3 = 8$) would be wasting ressources.

In figure 1|2–4 we can see how to arrive at a more efficient binary code (the Huffman code). First we list all the words according to their respective probabilities, starting at the bottom with the lowest. We then connect the two lowest probabilities by two converging lines from left to right and write the sum of them on the point where the two lines meet. In the first case, this is (.02 + .03 = .05), the probability of ('horse' or 'sells'). Now we look for the next two lowest probabilities and connect them accordingly, taking the sums we get into account as well. We proceed in this way until we have paths running from each word to one common point on the right, which is marked '1.00'. Now we simply label each upper path going left from a point '1' and each lower path '0'. The code for a word is then simply the sequence of binary digits encountered going left from the common point '1.00' to the word in question. As can be seen from figure 1|2–5, the average number of digits per word is 2.26, which is still larger than the entropy per

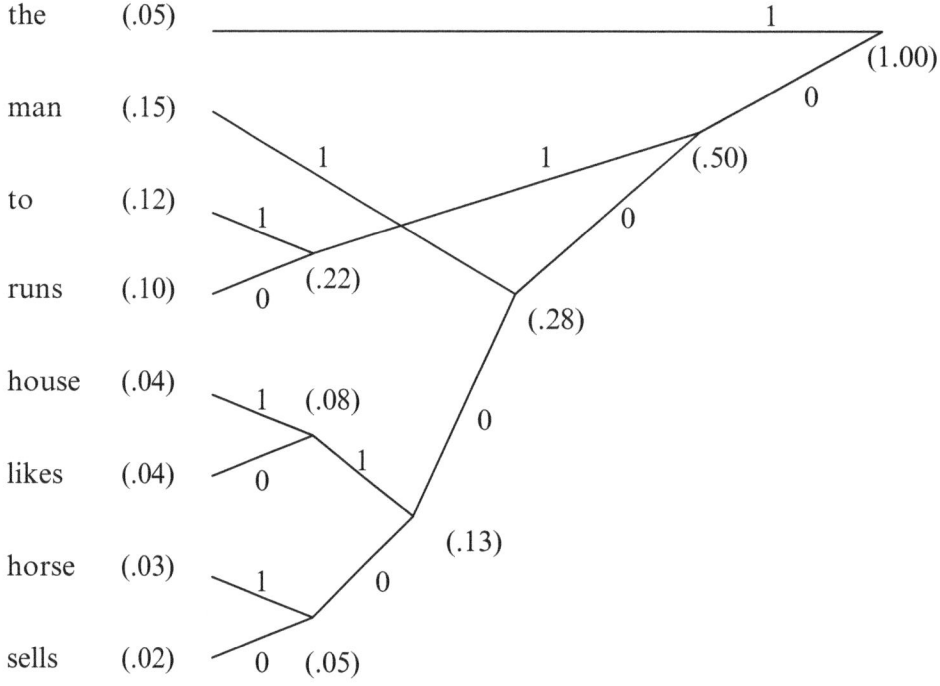

Figure 1|2-4

word, but better than 3 digits. If we consider sequences of words produced by the source, cut them into blocks, we can further approximate by this method the entropy, by making the blocks larger and larger.

As you know now, the statistical nature of *messages* depends on the source alone and is represented by a finite scheme, the way we did in the preceeding sections. But the statistical character of the *signal* that is eventually sent through a channel is determined by what we attempt to send through the channel *and* the specific capabilities of the channel to handle different signals. Depending on the technology we use, this capability will vary. Channels are in general *constrained*; they do not give us complete signal freedom. For example we have to take care that the symbols we chose to send through a channel are such that they are still recognizable at the receiving end.

However, for such a constrained channel there is a definte maximum of what can be achieved by the most efficient coding procedure.

Word	Probability	Code	Number of Digits in Code, N	Np
the	(.05)	1	1	.50
man	(.15)	001	3	.45
to	(.12)	011	3	.36
runs	(.10)	010	3	.30
house	(.04)	00011	5	.20
likes	(.04)	00010	5	.20
horse	(.03)	00001	5	.15
sells	(.02)	00000	5	.10
				2.26

Figure 1|2–5

> **Theorem 1|2–2 (Noiseless Channel)**
>
> Let a source have entropy H (bits per symbol) and a channel have a capacity C (bits per second). Then it is possible to encode the output of the source in such a way as to transmit at the average rate of $C/H - \varepsilon$ symbols per second over the channel where ε is arbitrarily small. It is not possible to transmit at an average rate greater than C/H.

In other words, if you devise a good code you can transmit symbols over a noiseless channel at an average rate as close to C/H as you like, but, no matter how clever the coding is, that average can never be made exceed C/H.

Noise and Equivocation

The communication system we have considered so far is still essentially incomplete, since we have not yet said anything about the reception of the messages. As you remember from the beginning of this chapter, the message may on its way be distorted by noise. Shannon's second fundamental theorem tells us to what degree we can get rid of noise by efficient coding procedures. *That* we can get rid of noise by means of coding is obvious. When we are in a noisy place and want to get a message through, we make it redundant, which can be done by adding gestures or saying the same thing twice. Doing this is costly, of course. Saying something twice takes double as much time as saying it only one time. So it is interesting to ask what the cheapest, i.e. most efficient codes can achieve given the presence of noise.

Let us begin with the entropy of a finite scheme, our source of m independent possible messages. We will call it 'S' for 'source'. The entropy is, as you might have guessed already, given by the standard formula (but we will change notation a bit to make things a bit more transparent. We will introduce $p(r)$ as the probability for the messages possible in R, and $p(s)$ for the probability of the particular messages in S):

$$H(S) = \sum_{s=1}^{m} -p(s)\log p(s)$$

At the other end of the channel we receive messages. Let us assume that here we also receive *m* possible messages. We will take the receiving end of the channel (we call it 'R') to be just another source with an entropy of its own

$$H(R) = \sum_{r=1}^{m} -q(r)\log q(r)$$

H(S) is clearly independent of *H(R)*, but *H(R)* depends on *H(S)*. If they were not so dependent, the situation would be hopeless. In such a case no information could come through. But *H(R)* does not only depend on *H(S)*, it also depends on the errors made in transmission.

Knowing the statistics of the message source and the statistics of the noisy channel, we can add the entropies the way we have learned it already ('*p(s,r)*' being the probability of the joint occurrence):

$$H(SR) = \sum_{s=1}^{m}\sum_{r=1}^{m} -p(s,r)\log p(s,r)$$

We have also learned to compute from here the conditional entropy for *R*, given that we know the message sent at *S* ('$p_s(\ )$' being the conditional probability on *s*, i.e. we know that *s* was sent)

$$H_S(R) = \sum_{s=1}^{m}\sum_{r=1}^{m} -p(s)p_s(r)\log p_s(r)$$

In case that we know the messages received, we can give the conditional entropy for the message source

$$H_R(S) = \sum_{r=1}^{m}\sum_{s=1}^{m} -p(r)p_r(s)\log p_r(s)$$

We can discern the following quantities: $H(S)$, being the entropy of the source, i.e. the uncertainty which message has been selected. $H(R)$ is the entropy produced at the receiver, i.e. the uncertainty which message will be received, given a source and a communication channel. $H(SR)$ is the uncertainty which of the possible messages at R will be received when a particular message at S was selected. $H_S(R)$ is the uncertainty of receiving r, when s was transmitted, it representes the average uncertainty of the sender as to what will be received, having sent the signal. $H_R(S)$ is the average uncertainty that s was sent, when r is received and represents the uncertainty of the receiver, having received the signal.

We also know that these quantities have certain relations:

$$H(SR) = H(S) + H_S(R)$$

This shows that the uncertainty of sending s and receiving r is the uncertainty of s plus the uncertainty of receiving r when s is sent. We also know that the following holds:

$$H(SR) = H(R) + H_R(S)$$

We see that when $H_S(R)$ is zero, $H_R(S)$ must also be zero and $H(R) = H(S)$. This is the case with a noiseless channel. The quantity $H_R(S)$, which is the uncertainty what was transmitted given a received signal, measures the amount of information lost in the channel. This quantity is also called *equivocation*.

Now, the rate of transmission of information over a channel is simply the entropy of the source minus the equivocation in bits per second. If O is the transmission rate, we have the following:

$$\begin{aligned} O = {} & H(S) - H_R(S) = \\ & H(R) - H_S(R) = \\ & H(S) + H(R) - H(SR) \end{aligned}$$

Now, the capacity of a noisy channel C is given by making O as large as possible for a given channel.

If the channel gets gradually noisier, we can make our transmission rates gradually slower to keep information flowing. If we also take larger and larger blocks of sequences of messages to encode them, we can approximate an equivocation of H − C. This is stated in the second fundamental theorem. We will not give the proof here since it will not be of much concern in the rest of the book. However, the notion of noise and equivocation will return in chapter 3|1.

> **Theorem 1|2–3 (Discrete Channel with Noise)**
>
> Let a discrete channel have the capacity C and a discrete source the entropy per second H. If $H \leq C$ there exists a coding system such that the output of the source can be transmitted over the channel with an arbitrarily small frequency of errors (or an arbitrarily small equivocation). If $H > C$ it is possible to encode the source so that the equivocation is less than $H - C + \varepsilon$ where ε is arbitrarily small. There is no method of encoding which gives an equivocation less than $H - C$.

Application to an example

To learn how Information theory can help you in real-world situation, consider the following case you might have encountered frequently already:

You have a balance and nine coins. Eight of the nine coins are of equal weight. The ninth, however, is of different weight (but it is unbeknownst to you whether it is lighter or heavier than the others.)

> *Problem:*
> *Develop a strategy to figure out by weighing only three times which coin differs in weight from the others and whether it is lighter or heavier than the others are.*

It seems reasonable to put always an equal number of coins onto the scales. In this case there are three possibilities:

1)   the left scale goes down

2)   the balance remains in equilibrium

3)   the right scale goes down

Hence, the highest amount of information you can receive by weighing once is log 3 = 1.58 bits (in this example we will choose the base 2 throughout, as we do in the rest of the book).

Now weighing three times can possibly create 4.74 bits of information. Being in the dark about (i.) which is the deviant coin and (ii.) whether it is lighter or heavier, you are asked to choose one possibility from a set of 18 equiprobable ones.

Maybe we should first check whether the problem is solvable at all. For this the information we can receive by weighing three times should be higher or equal to the information that corresponds to the 18 equiprobable outcomes. Luckily this is the case:

   log 18 = 4.16 bit < 4.74 bit

Unfortunately there is quite a number of ways how to put the coins onto the scales. Now we want to use information theory to develop a strategy.

It seems clever to get always the maximal information out of every single weighting. How much information do we gain from one weighting?

   Some definitions:

   Pl = Probability that the left scale goes down
   Pb = Probability that the scales remain in equilibrium
   Pr = Probability that the right scale goes down

Now we can apply our formula and see that the information gained by weighing once is

   $H = -(Pl \log Pl + Pb \log Pb + Pr \log Pr)$

We know, that H is at maximum if the probabilities are all equal. This strategy results in a simple rule: Weigh such that $Pl = Pb = Pr$ for each single case.

If we put n ($1 \leq n \leq 4$) coins onto the left scale and n onto the right, $9 - 2n$ coins will remain unweighed. In probabilities:

$Pb = (9 - 2n)/9$
$Pl = Pr = n/9$

If we want equiprobability, n has to be 3, so that $Pl = Pb = Pr = 1/3$.

Now, we mark all coins from 1 to 9. In the first step we put 1, 2, 3 onto the left scale and 4, 5, 6 onto the right. Now, either one of the scales goes down, or not. In case none goes down, we know that the weird coin is among 7, 8, and 9. Now we put 7, and 8 onto the scales and weigh a second time. It is easy to see that this leads to a solution.

Assume that after the first weighting the scales were not in equilibrium. Now we'll use only 4 of the 6 coins we used in the first weighting to keep the probabilities at 1/3 [$6 - 2 \times 2/6 = 1/3$]. To achieve this we have to move the weird coin with probability 1/2 from one scale to the other. We can do this easily:

Remove 1 and 4 from the scales.
Interchange 2 and 5.
Leave 3 and 6 where they are.

Now, after the second weighting we will have three possible outcomes:

1) The scales remain in equilibrium, hence coin 1 or 4 is the weirdo (and we simply weigh one of them with a normal coin).

2) If the scales are not in equilibrium but the situation is now inverted (other scale now up), 2 or 5 is the weirdo (and we simply weigh one of them with a normal coin).

3) If the scales are not in equilibrium, but the situation remains the same (same scale is up), 3 or 6 is the weirdo (and we simply weigh one of them with a normal coin).

The Relevance of MCT for a Semantic Theory

With respect to Shannon's theory, we can summarize the following:

 The theory deals with the average amount of information produced by a source, not with the amount of information carried by a single signal (but it's not so complicated to get there, as we shall see).

 The theory connects the analysis of information with the reduction of uncertainty.

 The theory does not, however, analyze the content of information carriers. It deals solely with the engineering problem.

Shannon, Weaver and others have nevertheless often talked as if parts of the theory would also apply to semantical problems. Most of this was certainly caused by the confusion of illustrating metaphors with the intended domain of application (similar to the confusion of thermodynamics with information theory as was discussed in the last chapter). Bar-Hillel has written an instructive paper 'An Examination of Information Theory' (Bar-Hillel 1955) where he uncovers these confusions.

MCT was the first attempt to explicate an aspect of information in mathematical terms. Even nowadays some people claim that it is the only aspect that is mathematically explicated so far, as for example in this quote by Tom Schneider:

> Information and uncertainty are technical terms that describe any process that selects one or more objects from a set of objects. We won't be dealing with the meaning or implications of the information since nobody knows how to do that mathematically. (Schneider 2003)

That 'nobody' knows how to deal with meaning, implication and the like mathematically, is fortunately false. If you read the book to the end, you will be among the people who indeed know how to do that.

Further Reading

A good introduction to MCT is:

- John R. Pierce, *An Introduction to Information Theory. Symbols, Signals and Noise*, New York 1980.

If you are interested in the mathematics covered, you will find quite a number of good introductions, most of which give the same proofs anyway, just visit your university library and pick one you like. We have followed the way Khinchin (1957) presents matters.

1│3   Algorithmic Information Theory

With the classical syntactic approach we have seen some ways to treat information and the flow of information syntactically. Claude Shannon's approach was related to the technical matters of his day (i.e. the telephone net and communication channels). Syntax came into view since the question had to be thought about how signs considered as *physical tokens* could be transmitted efficiently.

Today another syntactic approach is prominent: Gregory Chaitin's Algorithmic Information Theory ('AIT' for short).

It is related to matters of computer programming, i.e. it too is related to technical matters of its day. Syntax comes into view in this approach not because we consider signs as tokens, but because signs are considered as *generated strings* of signs/symbols. [We use 'sign', 'symbol' interchangeably here.] The generating of symbol strings falls within syntax. A grammar of a language is a way to generate strings of symbols from a given set of symbols by rules of transformation. The strings become interpreted in semantics, but the mere building of them – whether in correspondence to semantical rules or not – falls within syntax. The same holds for computer or programming languages. Furthermore we can consider programs which generate strings as their main task. We then consider a string as the syntactic output of a syntactic procedure.

Algorithmic Information Theory is a theory of informational content, not a theory of information flow. (It is not concerned with channels of transmission or the internet.) It deals with word strings. The basic measure is the same like in the original syntactic approach: bits. AIT, however, focuses not simply on the coding scheme of a given string, but on matters of generating that word string by a program. It is related to complexity theory (that is the theory of how much effort it takes to compute something).

Informational Content (Outline)

A string has some measure in bits. Usually this is the measure of memory space needed to store it. The measure increases with the length of the string. We can say string s has length n bits.

> **Definition 1|3–1**
>
> The informational content of a string is the length of the shortest program (in bits) which is needed to generate this very string.

The length of the shortest program for a string is also its complexity (the minimal effort we have to invest to get the string).

[For practical purposes Chaitin uses a version of LISP to give a working model of AIT. We will not go into programming details here.]

What is the theory behind Definition 1|3–1? Why should we look at a generating program and not at the string itself? Let us go into details then! A finite string of length n can be 'programmed' by having it simply printed. If k is the length in bits of the minimal program to print a string, then $n+k$ is the length of a program to generate the string. The program is nothing else than having the print instruction applied to a representation of the string itself in the code of its generating program. So any string can be generated, but the length of the program is not shorter than the string itself. We have gained nothing (e.g., in saving storage space) by having this program as compared to the string itself.

A further problem besides gaining nothing in case of finite strings is infinite strings. By the method of having a printing program we cannot generate them, since this would require a program of infinite size! You cannot have a program of infinite size stored, but it is logically possible to have a finite program running for an indefinite or even infinite time.

What we are looking for are programs that generate strings such that the size of the generating program is (considerably) less than the size of the string generated. If there is such a program we measure the informational content of a string by a number (considerably) less than the length of the string in bits. As the generating program gets smaller and smaller the string, by Definition 1|3–1, gets voider and voider of information. A string of 10 billion '1's printed in a row has (taking a suitable binary representation) a length of 10 billion bits. The program

```
int x := 0;
while (x < 10000000001)
    {   print '1';
        x := x + 1;}
```

has considerably less length. The string of 10 billion '1's is obviously boring and not informative. The longer the program to generate a string is the more irreducible structure has to be in the string generated. The repetition of '1's in the example string is a structure that can be reduced by a program very easily. If some part of a string cannot be reduced that easily the corresponding program has more lines to generate it. Therefore this string carries more information. The information in the string blocks further simplification of the program. A string that cannot be reduced by these means at all, therefore, carries maximal information!

> **Definition 1|3–2**
>
> A string is random if the size of the shortest program for it, if there is any, is not shorter than the string itself.

For a random string the shortest program to generate it, if there is any, is the print program mentioned in the last paragraph. The length of the print program is greater than the length of the string itself. The parenthesis 'if there is any' in definition 2 refers to strings of infinite lengths. Since there can be no print program for a string of infinite size, random strings of infinite size have no program to generate them at all.

Most strings are random, since there are far more strings than there are well-formed programs. Whatever your programming language may be it is defined what counts as a well formed line of code in that language, and what counts as a well formed program (i.e. one that is able to be executed). Say you use the language C. The vast majority of strings of symbols of our ordinary alphabet will not be a program in C. So given a length of a string n, most of the strings n long will not be programs in C. Since there is at most *one* string produced by each program, there are not enough programs of that size or a smaller size around to produce all the strings. The more complex a class of programs is (i.e. the greater the measure k of their length) the more not well formed programs of that size are there (i.e. the ratio of working programs to strings of that size to be generated by some program of that size gets worse and worse).

There are 2^n strings of length n (in binary code). There are less than 2^{n-k} programs of length less than $n - k$. Thus the number of strings of length n and complexity less than $n - k$ decreases *exponentially* as k increases. So the great majority of strings of length n are of complexity (resp. informational content) very close to n.

The mere fact that there are random strings is remarkable. Although every finite string can be generated by a program (so is computable) the effort of programming as compared to printing may not be worth it. We have just seen that this applies in fact to the majority of strings!

Formal Presentation

We can express these findings more generally. An abstract computer is an automaton that outputs some string given some input program. Let 'lg( )' denote the function that measures the length of a string in bits.

> Definition 1|3–3
>
> A computer is a partial recursive function $C(p)$. Its argument is a binary string. The value of $C(p)$ is the binary string output by C given the program p. If $C(p)$ is undefined the computation does not halt.

> Definition 1|3–1′
>
> The informational content $I_c(s)$ of a binary string s is defined to be the length of the shortest program p that makes the computer C

ALGORITHMIC INFORMATION THEORY

> output s, i.e.
>
> $$I_c(s) = \min \lg(p) \quad \text{(for } p \text{ with } C(p)=s\text{)}$$

> **Definition 1|3–2'**
>
> A random binary string s is a string having the property $I_c(s) \approx \lg(s)$.

Given these definitions we can express what we said about the printing program as

> **Theorem 1|3–1**
>
> There is a constant c such that $I_c(s) \leq \lg(s) + c$ for all s.

And what was said about the ratio of random strings to reducible strings can be expressed (very weakly) by

> **Theorem 1|3–2**
>
> There are less than 2^n binary strings of complexity less than n.

Theorem 1|3–2 just tells us that there are random strings. In fact most are, but by a further formal result it turns out hard to tell which strings are the random ones:

Suppose you want to know whether a given string is random. Can you prove it to be so? Say you want to find 'the first string of length 1000000000 that can be proven to be of complexity greater than 1000000000'. There is always a program $\log(n+c)$ bits long that can calculate the first string that can be proven to be of complexity greater than n. This program works as a proof checker: It looks through the list of strings with their corresponding generating programs, sees that the program really generates the string and by measuring the length of the program can deliver to us the program and the string of the length we look for (i.e. a program just one bit longer than the number we are looking for, with a corresponding string of just that complexity). Given some input number *n* the checking program is able to output a string of that length with a complexity greater than *n*. This checking program, however large it may be, has a finite size *c* itself. Given this program and very large *n* the test code's length, $\log(n+c)$, will be less than *n*. So there would be a program (viz. the checking program) of length less than *n* that gives as the output that string which is said to have no program of length less than *n*! That is absurd – such a string cannot exist. This means that we cannot compute the first string of some complexity measure, the first string with a specific amount of information (at least not for large *n*). For all sufficiently great values of *n* it cannot be proven that a *particular* string is of complexity greater than *n*, although there have to be many strings with that property. Thinking of checking program-size complexity as a (total) computable function is impossible:

> **Theorem 1|3–3**
>
> Program-size complexity is *uncomputable*.

Since program-size complexity is the measure of informational content, Theorem 1|3–3 says that for large *n* at least we cannot effectively specify a string with *n* bits of information.

Given this result we arrive at a sort of *incompleteness*: We can think of the proof checker of length *c* as being applied to proofs starting from *n* bits of axioms. Theorem 1|3–3 then says that for such a system consisting of a set of axioms and a proof checker it is impossible to prove that a particular binary string is of complexity $n+c$. So there are truths (i.e. facts about complexity resp. informational content) which cannot be proven. For some formal systems with *n* bits of axioms it is possible to determine each string of complexity less than $n+c$ and the complexity of each of these strings. And it is possible to exhibit each string of complexity greater than n, without being able to know *how much* the complexity of each of these strings exceeds n. Giving the strings of complexity less or equal to n is done by just giving the axioms so that one can start proving strings. Although the proofs might be very long, given the existence of a proof checker of length c the proof checker can check whether a given string was proved. If there is no proof from the axioms available the complexity of the input string must be greater than n. But we cannot say, by the means available in the system, how much the complexity exceeds that of n.

A Second Complexity Measure

Algorithmic Information Theory introduces a second complexity measure, i.e. a second measure of informational content. It concerns all the programs which compute a string s.

Consider the probability that a program the binary code of which was produced by coin tossing (using 'heads' for a '1', 'tails' for a '0') generates string s. Of course this probability is very low, since most programs produced thus are mere gibberish. AIT defines that probability as:

$$P(s) = \sum_{C(p)=s} 2^{-|k|}$$

this means that each program of length k generating s adds 2 to the minus k to the algorithmic probability of s.

Given this algorithmic probability further properties of it and of algorithmic informational content can be investigated within AIT, for example: relative complexity of two strings, mutual complexity or algorithmic independence. We will not go into the details here.

 The basic idea that you should remember is that of algorithmic informational content with its foundation in the idea of programs generating strings (i.e. Definitions 1|3–1, 1|3–1').

Further Reading

Chaitin has written several books and lots of papers on AIT, most of which are available online (http://www.umcs.maine.edu/~chaitin/). See, for example:

- *The Unknowable*, New York (Springer) 1999. [a popular overview]

- *Algorithmic Information Theory*, Cambridge (CUP) 1997³.

- *Information, Randomness and Incompleteness*. (World Scientific) 1990². [a collection of his papers]

2 | The Semantic Approach to Information
What Information is given by that Sentence?

THERE was a bridge party at Mr. Shaitana's elegant flat, with Dr. Roberts, Anne Meredith, Mrs. Lorrimer, and Major Despard participating; Shaitana was the host and only kibitzed. When the last rubber was finished and the guests were looking for Shaitana to take leave of him, they found him murdered, stabbed with a slender dagger. Every one of the four players had been the dummy at one time or another and had left the room for refreshments. Each one had, on the available evidence, an equal opportunity for murdering Shaitana, additionally all of them had a motive.

A reward was promised to those who could forward information leading to the identification of the murderer. A day later, Colonel Race, came and produced evidence sufficient to prove that Dr. Roberts could not have been the murderer. The next day Superintendent Battle showed, to the district attorney's satisfaction, that Anne Meredith was innocent. The following day, Mrs. Ariadne Oliver did the same for Mrs. Lorrimer. Whereupon Major Despard was duly convicted and imprisoned.

The problem now for the district attorney was how the reward should be distributed; he obviously had to adopt some numerical distribution. Since all informants eventually helped to find the murderer, he considered an equal share for all of them. He was not 100% confident with his solution, though, and discussed the case with his friend Poirot, a hobby mathematician. Poirot suggested to distribute the reward according to the information that each deposition contributed.

But what is the amount of information that the depositions contributed? If Mrs. Ariadne Oliver had just stated 'Major Despard is the murderer.' and Superintendent Battle had said 'Major Despard or Mrs. Lorrimer is the murderer.', Mrs. Ariadne Oliver's statement had clearly carried more information than Superintendent Battle's. And it seems that in some way something like this even happened, although both made statements that – taken in isolation – seem to carry the same amount of information (Superintendent Battle's statement 'Anne Meredith is innocent.' and Mrs. Ariadne Oliver's statement 'Mrs. Lorrimer is innocent.').

It seems that the latter statement could carry more information *for the attorney*, than the former, because it came in later, after the attorney knew already that the murderer was either Major Despard or Mrs. Lorrimer. But is the numerical amount of this information really greater than the numerical amount of 'Anne Meredith is innocent.'? The attorney did not receive this information in isolation either, for he knew already that Dr. Roberts is innocent. How can the numerical amount of such information be measured and compared?

The informants used sentences to give evidence. Somewhere in these sentences the expression 'is the murderer' occurred. It contributed to the information they provided *by its meaning*. The channel capacity of Mrs. Oliver – if you allow this way of talking about her – is not the point here, neither a prearranged coding scheme for this special case at hand provided by the superintendent Battle. In this story it is crucial that they convey information by sentences because of these sentence's (conventional) meaning.

2|1   Explicating Information by Possible Worlds

Introduction

Rudolf Carnap's and Yehoshua Bar-Hillel's contribution to the theory of information is usually neglected. The two prominent introductions to the philosophy of Carnap do not address Carnap's work in this area at all (Mormann 2000, Krauth 1970, Krauth does not even mention Carnap's work on semantic information in his list of Carnap's works, nor in his bio-bibliographical overview). Carnap himself, in his intellectual autobiography, is similarly reluctant (he sweeps over it in six sentences while discussing his work in inductive logic (Carnap 1963, 76)). Nevertheless, Carnap's contribution was quite influential and it started the topic this book is all about, the theoretical treatment of semantic information. In this chapter we will characterize his main ideas and show how it connects with the mathematical theory of communication developed in the first chapter.

Rudolf Carnap was born in 1891 in Ronsdorf, a small place close to Wuppertal and Cologne in Germany. After studying with the great mathematician and philosopher Gottlob Frege in Jena, and under the influence of the philosophy of Bertrand Russell, he became in 1926 a member of the so called Vienna Circle, a philosophical discussion group of (mainly natural) scientists lead by the Viennese philosophy professor Moritz Schlick. Carnap was one of the most prominent figures of the Vienna Circle. In general, when a history of philosophy textbook ascribes a certain view to 'the logical positivists' or 'the Vienna Circle' it had better ascribed the view to Carnap.

In 1935 the influence of Germany's Nazi Regime on Middle Europe became so unpleasant that Carnap had to emmigrate to the United States. There he worked at Harvard and Chicago, Santa Fe, Illinois, Princeton and the UCLA. In the early 50's, while being in Chicago and Princeton, he worked with Yehoshua Bar-Hillel at Harvard on semantic information.

Bar-Hillel, who originally came from Vienna, emmigrated to Palestine already in 1933 and had studied at the Hebrew University of Jerusalem. In the early 50's he was a research scholar at the M.I.T. Research Laboratory for Electronics. He is well known as a philosopher of science, logic and of language. When Bar-Hillel met Carnap in the winter 1950/51 in Chicago, Carnap directed his attention to Wiener's *Cybernetics* (Wiener 1948) and Shannon/Weaver's MCT.

Based on the work Carnap had done already in inductive logic (Carnap 1950), they developed a first theory of semantic information, an outline of which will be the topic of this chapter.

Sentences, not symbols

The first thing to note about the theory of semantic information is that Carnap and Bar-Hillel try to analyze the *content* and the *amount* of information as it is carried by *sentences* (linguistic entities) or *propositions* (nonlinguistic entities, expressed by sentences), rather than the average amount of information produced by a source via choices between different symbols.

Nevertheless, they hint already at a reduction to apply their analysis to the information carried by physical types or tokens: instead of talking about the information carried by a sound wave, one could instead talk about the information carried by the sentence:

(S)   'The sound wave ... has been transmitted.'

From the beginning, Carnap and Bar-Hillel emphasize that their theory should be understood as making certain simplifying assumptions. It is a theory of information that idealizes away from all pragmatic aspects and cognitive limitations:

> The semantic information carried by a sentence with respect to a certain class of sentences may well be regarded as the 'ideal' pragmatic information which the sentence would carry for an 'ideal' receiver whose only empirical knowledge is formulated in exactly this class of sentences. By an 'ideal' receiver we understand, for the purpose of this illustration a receiver with a perfect memory who 'knows' all of logic and mathematics together with any class of empirical sentences, all of their logical consequences. (Carnap/Bar-Hillel 1952: 223-224)

A Specimen Language and Some Definitions

For technical reasons, Carnap and Bar-Hillel (CBH, for short) develop their theory relative to restricted language systems of a certain type. The language systems they characterize are applied first-order language-systems with identity. CBH are aware of the fact that these systems are too restricted to allow a generalization of their results to all sciences, since not all science could be adequately translated into language systems with such a restricted expressive power. The main problem that comes to mind is the translation of scientific statements involving quantities such as mass, temperature and the like. Such statements need to be represented in a language containing functors, which the considered restricted systems lack.

Let's see how such systems are formally characterized. To make the presentation as easy to follow as possible we will be concerned with a very restricted specimen language only, the language L_3^2. The vocabulary of our specimen language consists of the following components:

(i) the customary logical connectives:

$$\equiv, \supset, \neg, \wedge, \vee$$

(ii) three names

a, b, c

(iv) two primitive predicates

M, Y

By definition we introduce the abbreviation for '¬M', and '¬Y', 'F' and 'O'. The interpretation for this language is given by the standard meaning for the logical connectives, namely equivalence, material implication, negation, conjunction and disjunction, and the following little story: Imagine a census is taken in a small village. In fact the village is so small that it contains only three inhabitants. Moreover, the census is even very restricted in scope, the census taker is only interested in whether the inhabitants are male or female, young or old (defined, respectively, as being younger than 35 years of age, and otherwise). Thus the three names of our specimen language, name the individuals living in the village in fixed order and the primitive predicates the properties Male and Young (by definition 'F' and 'O' name the properties Not-Male and Not-Young).

The *basic statements/sentences* of our language are built by a predicate letter followed by a name. 'Ma' is an example for a basic statement. All basic statements are expressions of our language. With the help of the logical connectives we can construct more statements:

If 'A' is a statement of our language, then '¬A' is also a statement of our language. If 'A' and 'B' are statements, so are 'A∨B', 'A∧B', 'A⊃B', 'A≡B'. Nothing else is a statement of our language. Thus with this language we can express that a is young and male, b male or c female, a young or old by 'Ya∧Ma', 'Mb∨Fc', 'Ya∨Oa'. Thus far everything should be familiar from a logic course.

We will now introduce a notion that is of some importance for semantic information theory, the notion of a state description:

Definition 2|1–1

State-description $=_{df}$ A conjunction of basic statements which contains for every possible basic statement of the language either this statement or its negation, but not both, and no other statement.

Such a state description in our language L_3^2 is

(S1)   Ma∧Ya∧Fb∧Yb∧Mc∧Oc

(S1) obviously gives a complete description of a possible state of the universe of individuals with respect to all properties and relations expressed by predicates of the system. This state-description describes our specimen universe completely. Any statement which logically implies and is stronger than a state-description is self-contradictory. A state description is the strongest synthetic statement in its language.

Since our specimen language L_3^2 is so weak, we can wonder how many state-descriptions can be build with the predicates and names at

	Mx∧Yx	Mx∧Ox	Fx∧Yx	Fx∧Ox		Mx∧Yx	Mx∧Ox	Fx∧Yx	Fx∧Ox
1.	a, b, c	-	-	-	33.	b	-	-	a, c
2.	-	a, b, c	-	-	34.	a	-	-	b, c
3.	-	-	a, b, c	-	35.	-	c	-	a, b
4.	-	-	-	a, b, c	36.	-	b	-	a, c
5.	a, b	c	-	-	37.	-	a	-	b, c
6.	a, c	b	-	-	38.	-	-	c	a, b
7.	b, c	a	-	-	39.	-	-	b	a, c
8.	a, b	-	c	-	40.	-	-	a	b, c
9.	a, c	-	b	-	41.	a	b	c	-
10.	b, c	-	a	-	42.	a	c	b	-
11.	a, b	-	-	c	43.	b	a	c	-
12.	a, c	-	-	b	44.	b	c	a	-
13.	b, c	-	-	a	45.	c	a	b	-
14.	c	a, b	-	-	46.	c	b	a	-
15.	b	a, c	-	-	47.	a	b	-	c
16.	a	b, c	-	-	48.	a	c	-	b
17.	-	a, b	c	-	49.	b	a	-	c
18.	-	a, c	b	-	50.	b	c	-	a
19.	-	b, c	a	-	51.	c	a	-	b
20.	-	a, b	-	c	52.	c	b	-	a
21.	-	a, c	-	b	53.	a	-	b	c
22.	-	b, c	-	a	54.	a	-	c	b
23.	c	-	a, b	-	55.	b	-	a	c
24.	b	-	a, c	-	56.	b	-	c	a
25.	a	-	b, c	-	57.	c	-	a	b
26.	-	c	a, b	-	58.	c	-	b	a
27.	-	b	a, c	-	59.	-	a	b	c
28.	-	a	b, c	-	60.	-	a	c	b
29.	-	-	a, b	c	61.	-	b	a	c
30.	-	-	a, c	b	62.	-	b	c	a
31.	-	-	b, c	a	63.	-	c	a	b
32.	c	-	-	a, b	64.	-	c	b	a

Figure 2|1–1

our disposal. The answer is easy to compute for a language L_n^π; with n being the number of names and π being the number of primitive predicates, there are $2^{\pi n}$ state-descriptions. Thus in our language L_3^2, there are $2^{3\times 2}$ state-descriptions, consequently 64. A list of all of them is given in Figure 2|1–1. Knowing that a, b and c are living in the village, and knowing what census he is going to take (which predicates he uses), the census taker knows before he even comes to the village, that the village is in one of the 64 states.

Another important notion we need to define is the notion 'range of a sentence'. We will first state the definition and then explain the notion with an example.

Definition 2|1–2

A possible world $=_{df}$ the semantic closure of a state description [given the language].

Definition 2|1–1

Range of B, R(B) $=_{df}$ For any sentence B of the system, the class of those possible worlds in which B holds.

Consider the sentence

(S2) Ma∧Ya∧Fb∧Yb

(S2) says that a is male and young, and that b is female and young. What the sentence does not talk about is what is the case with c. (S2) is obviously true in a state-description, e.g. it is true in state-description 9. But since (S2) leaves open whether c is young or old, male or female, (S2) is also true in 25, 42, and 53. Logically speaking, (S2) is *implied* by the state-descriptions 9, 25, 42, and 53. The class of these state-descriptions is the range of (S2). The range of (S2) contains 4 state-descriptions. As you can verify yourself, the range of

(S3) MaνYaνFbνYbνFcνOc

contains 63 state-descriptions. (One way to verify this is to note that (S3) is equivalent to '¬(Fa∧Oa∧Mb∧Ob∧Mc∧Yc)' which is the negation of state-description 52).

Analyzing Content

Given these definitions we can begin to explicate what the content of a sentence is. What a sentence A says, is that the universe is not in one of those states which are described by the Z (class of state descriptions) in $V_z - R(A)$, where V_z is the class of all Z. Thus (S3) says that the universe is not in state 52. In other words: A L_π^n-implies the negation of every Z in $V_z - R(A)$. These negations are called the content-elements E of A and their class the content of A, *Cont*(A).

Definition 2|1–4

Content-element for any sentence A $=_{df}$ Negation of a Z (state description) in $V_z - R(A)$, V_z being the class of all Z.

Definition 2|1–5

Cont(A) for any sentence A $=_{df}$ Class of all content-elements E of A.

An analytic statement has minimum content, and a self-contradictory statement maximum content. In Bar-Hillel's words:

> A self-contradictory statement tells too much, it excludes too much, and is incompatible with any state of the universe, whereas an analytic statement excludes nothing whatsoever and is compatible with everything. (Bar-Hillel 1964, 301)

According to the scholastic dictum, *omnis determinatio est negatio*, that we have encountered already, the content of a sentence is taken to be the class of those possible states of the universe (state-descriptions) which are excluded by this sentence. In other words, the class of those states whose being the case is incompatible with the truth of the statement/sentence. This again is an expression of the inverse relationship principle that we have discussed in the very first chapter (1|1) of this book.

Quantifying Information

Remembering the second chapter (1|2) of the book, the amount of information carried by a signal was the quantity Shannon was interested in. In the semantic theory we want to have something similar. The best we can say at the moment is that a certain statement has a larger content than another one, in the case in which the class of state-descriptions excluded by the first statement includes the class of state-descriptions excluded by the second one as a proper part. In our specimen language we would say that

$$Cont(\text{'Ma'}) > Cont(\text{'Ma}\vee\text{Yb'}),$$

since the class of state-descriptions excluded by 'Ma' contains the class of state-descriptions excluded by 'Ma∨Yb'. But if two contents are exclusive like in the case of 'Ma' and 'Mb∨Yb', we still want to say that the one conveys more information than the other one does, although the set of state-descriptions excluded by the former sentence does not include the set of state-descriptions excluded by the latter sentence. The solution chosen by CBH is to define measure functions over the set of contents.

Carnap could provide these from his explication of logical probability. The basic intuition behind this use of measure functions is this: the greater the logical probability of a statement, the smaller its content measure. CBH go on to define measure functions over ranges, one of which, m_p is supposed to be the logical probability on no evidence. The logical probability of a sentence A is 1 iff A is L-true and 0 iff A is L-false. The content measure of A, $cont(A)$, is by definition the logical probability of $\neg A$, $m_p(\neg A)$. The choice of this very function can easily be motivated: there is one clear adequacy criterion for a proper m-function, the greater the logical probability of a statement, the smaller its content measure.

Now, the mathematically simplest relationship that fulfills this requirement is obviously the complement to 1. Let $m_p(A)$ be the logical probability of A. Then $1 - m_p(A)$ can be taken as the plausible measure for the content of A!

Definition 2|1–6

The content measure of a sentence A, $cont(A) =_{df} 1 - m_p(A)$.

But another intuition we have is that something like the following should hold for inductively independent statements A and B (remember our discussion of entropy in 1|2):

$$cont(A \wedge B) = cont(A) + cont(B)$$

Since *cont* is not additive under inductive independence (as we shall see in a minute), we need another explicatum for amount of information that will have this property. What the alternative is supposed to do is to assign to 'Ma∧Yb', for instance, an information measure that is equal to the sum of the information measures of 'Ma' and 'Yb', since these two statements are inductively independent. If, under a particular normalization, the information measure of each of these two statements turns out to be one (bit), we would like the information measure of their conjunction to be 2. The additivity of *cont* cannot help us. Both statements 'Ma' and 'Yb', although inductively independent, are not content exclusive. And *cont* is additive only if the sentences are content exclusive, i.e. if no state-description is excluded by both sentences. But both imply the statement 'Ma∨Yb', which excludes all state-descriptions in which 'Fa∧Ob' is the case. And such state descriptions exist, 27 is one of them. Thus we need another measure for amount of information that gives us the additivity we want.

An Alternative Content Measure and Our Pre-explicatory Intuitions

If we, for simplicity, assume the in-value of each incoming basic sentence as being 1, we arrive at the following alternative formula for the amount of information, *inf*, for any sentence A:

Definition 2|1-7

$inf(A) =_{df} - \log m_p(A)$

Which is analogous to MCT (Mathematical Communication Theory) and the amount of information carried by a signal i. Now, *inf* allows for additivity in case of inductive independence, since it is logarithmic.

Another intuition is that the amount of information of any two statements should always be at most equal to the sum of the amounts of these statements. But whereas

$$cont(A \wedge B) \leq cont(A) + cont(B)$$

this does not hold for *inf*. 'John is hungry' carries different information when taken relative to the statement 'John is hungry', as evidence, i.e. when taken absolutely, as when taken relative to the statement 'John is thirsty'. We can account for this by adding the following definitions:

Definition 2|1-8

$inf(A|B) =_{df} inf(A \wedge B) - inf(B)$

We model relative information here, and take conditional probability as a model. The amount of information of some statement A relative to some statement B should be the same function of the probability of A given B as the absolute amount of information of A of the absolute probability of A. To fulfil this requirement means to have a log type of function.

> **Definition 2|1-9**
>
> $inf(A|B) =_{df} -\log m_p(A|B)$

in analogy to

$$inf(A) = -\log m_p(A)$$

where as it is not the case that

$$cont(A|B) = 1 - m_p(A|B)$$

Another of our pre-explicatory intuitions is the following: Asked what we regard as the appropriate relation between the absolute amount of information of a given statement A and its amount of information relative to any B, we are normally very positive that no increase in the evidence should increase the amount of information, though it might not necessarily decrease it. Now, it can be shown that

$$cont(A|B) \leq cont(A)$$

whereas the corresponding statement for *inf* does not hold. Intuitively, the difference is supposed to be this: Whereas *cont* might be viewed as a measure of the substantial information a statement carries, since this at most decreases, *inf* measures its surprise value, the prior unexpectedness of its truth, where the surprise value is dependent on further knowledge.

Consider our census example again. When the census taker learns that 'Ma' is true, he learns that the universe is not in any of certain 32 states out of 64 states it could possibly have been in. If it is the second thing he learns, having learned first that 'Fb' is true, the substantial increase about that universe is less.

'Ma' tells him only that the universe is not in any of certain 16 states from a set of 32 states it still could have been in (and these 16 states are a proper subset of the 32 states when his first information was that 'Ma' is true). On the other hand, although his knowledge now increases less substantially, he should now be more surprised than he was in the first case.

Knowing NOTHING, he expects a to be male as much as female, but having observed that b is female, he then expects a to be female rather than male and is therefore rightfully surprised when a turns out to be male after all.

$$cont(\text{'Ma'}|\text{'Fb'}) < cont(\text{'Ma'})$$

$$inf(\text{'Ma'}|\text{'Fb'}) > inf(\text{'Ma'})$$

Consider that we are about to perform an experiment with n possible outcomes and that one and only outcome must occur. What is the amount of information which the outcome of this experiment can be expected to carry? If we want on these grounds to define the expectation of information in a given situation in which we have a number of mutually exclusive alternatives with the logical probabilities p_i, we arrive at the by now familiar entropy expression:

$$-\sum_{i=1}^{n} p_i \log p_i$$

Let's summarize the relationships between *cont* and *inf*:

$$cont(A \wedge B) = cont(A) + cont(B)$$

iff (A∨B) is logically true;

$$inf(A \wedge B) = inf(A) + inf(B)$$

iff A and B are independent with respect to their logical probability.

$$inf(A) = cont(A) = 0$$

iff A is logically true.

More interesting are their differences, though:

$$cont(A|B) = cont(A \supset B)$$

$$inf(A|B) = -\log m_p(A|B)$$

This is one reason for the preference given in MCT to the correlate of *inf*. To figure out that there are more than one explicata for our prescientific concept of the amount of information a message carries, is not too surprising or problematic. Explications are meant to uncover exactly such prescientific confusions. Just as Carnap hit at two different concepts of probability in our prescientific notion of probability, he here revealed two notions of content measure behind our pre-scientific notion of that.

Summary
The theory of semantic information is the birth of epistemic and doxastic logic within the possible worlds framework. Possible worlds became later what are the state descriptions in Carnap's and Bar-Hillel's theory.

Of course, this theory idealizes away from many factors that determine the subjective amount of information that a sentence carries in actual situations. Even if we restrict our language to the finite set of names there are and the predicates of L_2^3, the basic statement 'George W. Bush is female' subjectively carries more information than the basic statement 'Arnold Schwarzenegger is male' (in California, given politically correct first names, Carnap's measure functions deliver correct results). These problems are partly due to the fact that Carnap's measure for the amount of information a sentence carries is supposed to be determinable a priori. But we never get confronted with statements so isolated from any synthetic knowledge we have. Thus, usually, a statement carries a different amount of information, simply because we had some prior information already. Carnap tried to account for that by his relative measures (*inf*(A|B); *cont*(A|B)). In the next chapter we will discuss an alternative approach that could be considered a further development of Carnap's ideas.

Further Reading
For a good overview one could read

- Yehoshua Bar-Hillel. 'Semantic Information and its Measures', in: *Transactions of the Tenth Conference on Cybernetics*, New York 1952, 33-48.

A critical discussion of the a priori assignment of measure functions and an extension of the CHB approach to the relational case is presented in

- Jaakko Hintikka. 'On Semantic Information', in: J. Hintikka / P. Suppes (eds.), *Information and Inference*, Dordrecht 1970, 3-27.

2|2 Strong Semantic Information

The semantic approach of Carnap and Bar-Hillel gives us an account of information of declarative sentences, distinguishing between information (as modelled by a set of possible worlds) and a quantitative measure of informational content. The model, however, has serious side effects.

 Firstly it assigns (by it's *a priori* measures of probability) the same probability to all contingent basic sentences making them carry – contra-intuitively – all the same information. That is a consequence of taking the probabilities as *logical* probabilities. If they had been taken as just some probability the explication of amount of information would have been linked to an *epistemic* concept (since one probability distribution had been preferred – supposedly on epistemic grounds involving knowledge of the world). Without that all contingent statements of the same logical structure carry the same amount of information. In isolation from world knowledge and semantic postulates fixing distinguished ranges for some sentences there is no measure of the *semantic* amount of information at all.

 Secondly it assigns all logically determined sentences (those sentences being either tautological or contradictory) one of two constant amounts of information (either 0 for a tautology or 1 in case of a contradiction); this means that logical truths carry no information and that contradictions carry maximal information. Once again this does not seem to be true. There seem to be quite different logical truths if you just look at different logical systems or just at the distinction between propositional and functional logic – why should all these truths carry no information at all? They do not seem to have the same meaning (see Chapter 2.3). And does a contradiction really give you maximal information? Contradictions are maximal given standard logic. Since *ex contradictione quodlibet*

(1) $A \wedge \neg A \supset B$

holds in standard logic, given any contradiction any sentence whatsoever can be derived, so given any contradiction any information can be derived, so contradictions give you – logically speaking – all information you can possibly get. A contradiction excludes all state description so the measure on the set of possible worlds excluded by its truth (a measure of informational content) will be maximal. Accordingly the probability of the contradiction $\bot$ is 0, thus taking informational content *cont* to be the reverse of probability $cont(\bot)=1$.

To overcome at least partially the second difficulty we take a look in this chapter on Lucinao Floridi's theory of *strong* semantic information. We will continue to discuss this problem in a wider context in the next chapter (Chapter 2|3).

Floridi baptizes the fact that contradictions are assigned maximal amount of information 'the Bar-Hillel/Carnap semantic paradox'. To dissolve the paradox information is linked to truth and truthlikeness. No measure of probability is involved.

The informational content of a sentence A or its *informativeness* is defined extensionally as a function of its deviation from the truth in the matter A talks about. Each sentence A corresponds to a situation *s* that is the case if A is true (respectively A is true if *s* is the case). In terms of a support relation between situations and sentences (or other carriers of information or units to be evaluated) we can write (see Chapter 4|1):

$s \vDash A$.

If *s* is the situation A describes, then A trivially is maximally informative with respect to *s*. The theory of strong semantic information now measures the informativeness of A by two factors:

(i)   the polarity of A (i.e. whether it is true or false) and

(ii) the *degree of discrepancy* between A and the given total state of the world

where the situation referred to by A or *some variant of that situation* is part of the actual situation (the actual world). Consider the following three statements:

(2) There are five people in the library.

(3) There are seven people in the library.

(4) There are seventeen people in the library.

Now there are five people in the library. That makes statement (2) true and the other two of them false. With respect to polarity there is no difference between (3) and (4), since both are false. Nevertheless we would say that (3) is *closer to the truth* than (4) is. (3) might even be closer to the truth than

(5) There is at least one person in the library.

since (3) *although being false* provides us with more specific content (rather close to the actual situation) whereas (5) does not. (5) is true whether there are five or five hundred people in the library.

The deviation of A from the truth is measured by a function f from sentences to some real value in the interval $[-1,1]$. If $f(A) = 0$ then there is no discrepancy at all, i.e. A is true and appropriately specific. A metric on the set of sentences may be derived by comparing them with each other how far they deviate from the truth and from each other (arriving at some *order* of accuracy), and a consequent assigning of numerical values. A metric on a given set of sentences should fulfil the following conditions (for a sentence A referring to a specific set of situations s_1):

(M1) $s_1 \vDash A \rightarrow f(A) = 0$

(M2) $(\forall s) s \vDash A \rightarrow f(A) = 1$

(M3) $\neg(\exists s)\, s \vDash A \rightarrow f(A) = -1$

(M4) $s_1 \vDash A \land \neg(s_1 \subseteq s_2) \land \text{Obtains}(s_2) \rightarrow (0 > f(A) > -1)$

(M5) $s_1 \vDash A \land s_2 \subseteq s_1 \land s_2 \vDash A \rightarrow (0 < f(A) < 1)$

(Taking the support relation to take sets of situations as relatum differs from the approach in Chapter 4|1, but makes the presentation easier here.)

Principle (M1) says that A is precise if it is supported by the situation being the case. A situation may support imprecise sentences – since we have, for example, sentences with existential quantification here. (M2) says that a sentence being true in all situations (i.e. a tautology) carries maximal deviation or discrepancy. We can conclude nothing about the world from a tautology so it is as far from giving positive information about a situation as one can get. (M3) says that if there is no (possible) situation at all that fits A, then (A being a contradictory statement) there is no information in A. The discrepancy of a contradiction is maximal since there is no other statement that could be further off the truth. A contradiction has the highest degree of semantic inaccuracy. (M3) expresses the requirement that the 'Bar-Hillel/Carnap paradox' should be avoided. (M4) says that in case the situation corresponding to a sentence does not obtain (i.e. it is not a part of the situation that is the case), then the sentence A has a negative discrepancy from the truth, since it is false, and it is not as deviant as a contradiction, since there is a possible situation that supports it. (M5) takes care of sentences like (5) which may be true but are very unspecific. The set of situations in which there are five people in the library is a subset of the set of situations in which there are any people in the library, so the information contained within that set is more specific, so a sentence like (5) that is still supported by a more specific set of sentences can only be a sentence exhibiting some imprecision that is positively measured (i.e. is greater than 0 and smaller than the maximal positive deviance of a tautology).

We can now define (semantical) equivalence of two sentences A and C as A and C having the same polarity and a comparable degree of semantic discrepancy with respect to the obtaining situation. A sentence is the more (positively) vacuous the more situations support it. (Given the function f the theory of strong semantic information can then introduce further concepts like the *degree* of semantic informativeness and the quantity of *vacuity* for each sentence A.)

Notwithstanding the details what should be obvious is that this theory allows for more fine grained distinctions between sentences of the same logical form than the Carnap/Bar-Hillel approach allows for. The measure of informativeness, however, is calculated with respect to the knowledge which situation does *in fact obtain*. The theory is, therefore, no theory of *a priori* semantic or informational content (for not logically determined statements). It is an *epistemic* theory of informational content in distinction to a real/pure semantic account of information, which is not relative to any world knowledge.

Further Reading
The exposition is based on Luciano Floridi's paper

 📖 'Outline of a Theory of Strongly Semantic Information', *Minds and Machines* 14 (2004), 197-221.

2|3 Do You Get Information in a Logic Course?

This chapter deals with a special problem within the field of explicating the/a concept of information: the problem of the informational content of logical truths. This chapter also uses some situation semantics, which will be introduced in chapter 4 and refers to Dretske's theory of information, which will be introduced in chapter 3 (however, you should be able to follow the discussion in this chapter already).

In several departments logic courses are taught and students there get to know things they did not know before. They learn something. And every time a researcher hears a talk by a colleague about some new system of logic or some new theorem he learns something. When she devises a proof herself of a new theorem she discovers something. So getting to know some logical truth seems to involve acquiring some information. This applies especially to drawing consequences. In drawing a consequence we get information about what was entailed or implied by what we already believed. Getting to know a consequence relation between some beliefs or sentences seems to be getting information.

Nevertheless the standard explications of informational content are not able to deal with the problem of assigning informational content to logical truths. We will highlight this problem in the different approaches. We then distinguish several strategies to deal with the problem, i.e. strategies to assign logical truth either informational content or some other quality accounting for the gain in knowledge upon acquiring them. Hintikka's solution will be presented, since he – although offering a solution that nobody took up and that has several shortcomings – was the first who tried systematically to deal with the problem. Some ways to look for a solution to the problem are hinted at, but none has been fully developed so far.

The Problem in the Syntactic Approach
Rational students should engage only in courses where they can learn something. Now, unfortunately, it seems that you can learn nothing in

a logic course, if learning something means to acquire some information, since the informational content of logical truths – seen in the light of the standard approaches to measuring or defining informational content – is: nothing!

Let us consider the mathematical theory of communication as developed by Claude Shannon (see Chapter 1|2) first:

The average information of a source is defined given some measure of the probability that some symbol out of a set of symbols occurs and the uncertainty with which that symbol occurs given the possible strings of symbols made out of the symbols in that set. Starting from some requirements on the notion of informational content (like information being additive and that information decreases uncertainty) Shannon uses a logarithmic measure of the uncertainty of a symbol, and a probability measure to derive his famous formula for the information carried by a message of n possible messages on average:

(1) $$H = -\sum_{i=1}^{n} p_i \log p_i$$

This refers to the source as a whole. Applied to a single signal we can say:

(2) $I(A) = \log(1/p(A))$

The amount of information in a single symbol A (whether letters in a word or sentences taken as the single units in talking) is the logarithm of the reverse of its probability.

Logical truths are not random. They can be completely expected, there are no alternatives to them. Their probability is 1. This means in the syntactic approach, given the definition of informational content 'I(x)', that we get for a logical truth A:

(3) $I(A) = \log(1/p(A)) = \log(1/1) = \log 1 = 0$

That means: Logical truths carry no information at all. You learn nothing from them!

The Problem in the Semantic Approach

Carnap and Bar-Hillel (see Chapter 2|1) developed a semantic theory of informational content within the possible worlds framework. Their analysis from the very beginning concerns sentences not individual letters or symbols. As usual one might identify what a sentence says with the set of possible worlds in which the sentence is true. The informational content of a sentence might be taken as the set of worlds excluded by this sentence being true, since so we keep the intuition that informational content is related to surprise that what a symbol says is the case. So Carnap and Bar-Hillel develop two explications of semantic content. One starts with the idea just mentioned and gives a more semantic measure of informational content, since the range of worlds excluded by a sentence is statically associated with that sentence. It does not change with our knowledge which world is the actual world. A measure *cont* can be gained by counting the excluded worlds or by employing an a priori probability measure which assigns all worlds the same probability. Let *m* be such a measure. $m(A)$ is the probability of a sentence A. Then we can define *cont*:

(4) $cont(A) = 1 - m_p(A)$

Logical truths are true in all possible worlds. The set of the worlds excluded by their truth is $\emptyset$, i.e. given the explication '*cont*( )' of informational content in the possible worlds approach:

(5) $cont(A) = \emptyset$ (collecting the excluded worlds) or

$cont(A) = 1 - m_p(A) = 1 - 1 = 0$

Given a probability measure on worlds the informational content of a logical truth A is the number of (the sum of the probability of) the worlds in $\emptyset$, i.e. 0, or the reverse of the probability of A, i.e. once again 0. Given *cont*, a logical truth carries no semantic information at all although logical truths are, given Carnap's semantic model, true because of their meaning!

Considering a different set of intuitions with respect to informational content, Carnap and Bar-Hillel provide a second explication of semantic content in terms of probability (given any probability distribution on the set of possible worlds) and a logarithmic measure. This second measure is more epistemic than semantic, since the probability distribution we choose might reflect our world knowledge. With this measure they derive a semantic analog to Shannon's formula:

(6) $inf(A) = - \log(m_p(A))$

Repeating the calculation from the last paragraph we get:

(7) $inf(A) = - \log(m_p(A)) = - \log 1 = 0$

Once again you learn nothing from logical truths!

Luciano Floridi (see Chapter 2|2) developed the semantic approach into a theory of 'strong semantic information'. His starting point is one of the contra-intuitive consequences of the original semantic approach: that contradictions have the maximum information value. This holds in the Carnap/Bar-Hillel framework since contradictions exclude all possible worlds; their range being ∅ means that the reverse of their range is the totality of possible worlds. Their probability is zero. And the reverse of their probability is therefore maximal. If A is a contradiction:

(8) $cont(A) = 1 - m_p(A) = 1 - 0 = 1$

(9) $inf(A) = \log(1/m_p(A)) = \log(1/0) \approx \log \infty = \infty$

Floridi calls this 'the Bar-Hillel/Carnap paradox', since intuitively we would say that somebody who utters a contradiction has said nothing at all, has conveyed no information at all. He develops a theory in which we not only consider the truth value of a sentence but also the amount of its deviation (in degrees) from the actual world (like 'there are eight dogs' deviates more from a situation with two dogs than 'there are six dogs', although both sentences are false). Given his account of discrepancy of a sentence from the actual world he can derive that the discrepancy of contradictions is maximal, which means that their informational content is zero. So he can in fact solve the problem of the supposedly informative contradictions. As one condition in the development of the appropriate informational content function, however, he explicitly lays down the condition that if A is a tautology it is assigned the maximum degree of discrepancy. That makes it a part of his framework that logical truths carry no information. Thus even this elaborated semantic approach refuses to give us information from logical truths.

The Problem in Dretske's Approach

Fred Dretske (see Chapter 3|1) developed an account of information that preserves the main ideas of the syntactic approach and tries to combine it with an externalist account of semantic informational content. It takes information as being out there in the world. Meanings might be partly in the head but information is not. Information flows because of the causal connections between some object a being F and another object b being G. Dretske does not consider average amounts of information associated with some symbol but an absolute content given a framework of natural laws and the circumstances of the situation. So a's being F carries the information that b is G if the conditional probability of b being G given a being F is 1. (A conditional probability of less than 1 will not do, because of some criteria on information flow like his famous 'Xerox-Principle'.) Knowledge is defined as the belief that a is F caused by the information that a is F, given some natural laws. The natural laws and so, of course, the laws of logic belong to the framework within which information flow is recognised. What belongs to the framework cannot carry information itself. Even natural laws, as given in all relevant contexts, 'have an informational measure of zero' (Dretske 1981, 264). Logical truths do not cause anyway. So in Dretske's externalistic approach to information the problem of non-contingent (logical) truth is even more pressing. Since you have the framework already you can learn nothing from a logical truth.

How to Solve the Problem?
There might be different types of solution:

(i) logical truths carry no information in the sense explained, but are nevertheless of interest because of some other quality.

This type of solution would leave information theory as it is but supplements it with a theory of what happens in recognising logical truths besides information flow as explained by the standard accounts.

(ii) information is analysed so as to be able to distinguish between some logical truths.

A kind of syntactic approach can be of type (i), an ontological approach of type (ii).

A Syntactic Solution
Within a semantic approach some syntactic features can be given a role:
  The logical truths

(10) $p \supset p$

and

(11) $(\forall x)(x=x)$

differ syntactically. Carnap's concept of *intensional isomorphy* (Carnap 1955) introduces some syntactic features into an account of meaning. Two sentences are intensionally isomorphic if one can be transformed into the other substituting step by step expressions of the same syntactic category for each other. Since (11) contains expression of the syntactic type individual (variable) it cannot be transformed into (10). We can introduce a concept of meaning that not only requires logical equivalence but also requires that two logically true sentences can only have the same meaning if at their deepest level of logical form they share one logical form (Bremer 1993, 295-96). So (10) and (11) differ in meaning! We care about differences in meaning so that would be an account why we care about different logical truths. Each logical truth tells us that some individual sentence (i.e. a sentence with a meaning that distinguishes it from all other sentences) is a logical truth. In recognising a consequence relation we see a connection between meanings that we did not see before.

Another version of such a syntactic solution could be developed within a computational theory of mind which refers to mental representations (maybe some language of thought symbols). Within such a computational theory of mind mental representations have their semantic features and their (psychological) role because of their syntactic features, since only these configurations enter into causal connections (cf. Fodor 1987, 1994).

The (mental) representations 'bachelor' and 'unmarried man' have different functional roles because of their syntax (cf. Dretske 1981, 214-19). We care about that! So an analytic truth like

(13) A bachelor is an unmarried man.

although carrying no information given Dretske's explanation of information is interesting since it connects two mental representations with a strong link which had not had that link before, if you did not know (13) before. A similar explanation applies to recognising consequences. These ideas on logical truths commit themselves to the representationalist/computationalist theory of mind and await further elaboration.

An Ontological Solution

Even given intensional isomorphy in a semantic approach incorporating syntactic features there are logical truths getting the same meaning although being distinct:

(14) $(\forall x)Raven(x) \supset (\exists x)Raven(x)$

and

(15) $(\forall x)Dog(x) \supset (\exists x)Dog(x)$

would be an example. According to the first syntactic approach mentioned (14) and (15) would have the same meaning. That could be acceptable, since what you learn in terms of logic from (14) you can learn from (15) as well. If you want to make a distinction between even these sentences you need more than logical form. To solve such cases an ontological solution might be needed which refers to the constituents (resp. the referents of the constituents). Such an ontological solution would incorporate a more fine grained carving up of sentences or their referents. If you do not care about ontological plenty, you can distinguish (14) and (15) since the one contains the property of being a dog while the other contains the property being a raven. Situation semantics (see Chapter 4) is such a fine grained approach. For example the infon $\langle\langle dog, fido, 1\rangle\rangle$ (Fido is a dog) and the infon $\langle\langle dog, hasso, 1\rangle\rangle$ (Hasso is a dog) are different infons, since the first involves the object Fido while the latter involves the object Hasso. An analysis of compound infons and a consequence relation can then establish the difference between (14) and (15). This kind of solution would involve heavy ontological commitment.

Hintikka's Approach

For mainly historical reasons let us take a look at Hintikka's approach. He was one of the first to address the problem as a problem of the informational content of logical truths. He considered the problem in the light of epistemic modal logic, questioning the correctness of two principles of epistemic modal closure. Epistemic modal logics (i.e. epistemic logics of the early kind, modelled after alethic modal logic) better be normal modal logics if there should be any logic of the epistemic operators at all.

Normal modal logics contain a rule of necessitation:

(16) $\vdash A \rightarrow \vdash \Box A$

and the K-Axiom:

(17) ⊢ □(A ⊃ B) ⊃ (□A ⊃ □B)

i.e. the derived rule:

(18) ⊢ (A ⊃ B) → ⊢ (□A ⊃ □B).

Without these there is not much of a logic of '□'.

The counterparts in epistemic modal logic (with a knowledge operator 'K') then are:

(19) ⊢ A → ⊢ KA   [all logical truths are known]

(20) ⊢ (A ⊃ B) → ⊢ (KA ⊃ KB)   [all consequences are known]

which are considered highly contra-intuitive. Imagine a little dialogue

    A: Why didn't you show up in the exam?
    B: I need not, I know all logical truths.
    A: Wow! How that?
    B: ⊢ A → ⊢ KA, you know from modal logic class, don't you?
    A: Then what about '◇(A ⊃ B) ∧ □A ⊃ ◇B'? From modal logic, right?
    B: Eerr??

Hintikka tries to avoid these contra-intuitive consequences by distinguishing kinds of information: *surface* vs. *depth information*. But he also restricts the closure principles.

Hintikka believes there is a sense of information in which logical inference can add to our information, i.e. our knowledge. His explication relates our problems in recognising a logical truth (i.e. in getting additional information) to the increasing depth of a procedure of checking quantificational consistency (in First Order Logic).

Surface and depth information are defined relative to a nesting of quantifiers.

Closure (under K) does hold only if A ⊃ B is a surface tautology at the depth of A (i.e. at the depth of what is already known). That is we look at the depth of quantification in A and the depth of quantification in B; if the depth of B does not exceed that of A, Hintikka sees no problem and closure under K should apply. If the depth of B is greater than that of A, closure under K cannot be applied automatically. When we learn A ⊃ B, we gain information (viz. the difference between surface and depth information). Increasing the depth and then detaching (in a conditional) can add to our knowledge. But closure (under K) does not apply here! An account of epistemic closure, therefore, depends on an account of logical depth information (in a first order possible worlds semantics).

Although it is difficult to explain all details of Hintikka's approach, we might get a feeling of his solution by looking at some details:

Depths informally concerns the finite number of individuals we consider at the same time respectively the number we need to define another individual (given a language L_i). We need some measure of surface and depth information to compare them. A bound variable does not refer to any individual in particular, but we can ask whether the definition of the individual concerned refers (by nested quantifiers) to other individuals. The degree of a formula is obtained as the sum of the number of free singular terms and the maximal number of quantifiers whose scopes have a common part in the formula (i.e. its depth). Quantifiers are pushed inwards. Depth depends on quantifier changes like '∃x∀y∃w∀v(...)' (depth 4, say), since '∃x∃y' could be simplified into a single quantifier (on a pair). We can count quantifiers and singular terms to recognise the depths and the degree (of the parts) of a formula.

Let a *Q-predicate* be the conjunction of all basic predicates of a language L_i or their negation as they apply to some individual. There are as many types of individuals as Q-predicates. We consider only types here. Given these predicates we describe a type of world by saying which Q-predicates are instantiated. These descriptions of types of worlds are *constituents*. They are consistent. If we also allow for basic relations, a Q'-predicate can be of more than depth 1. If we nest references to other individuals, depth increases, as does the depth of constituents.

These constituents now can be inconsistent, since they might refer to an individual which is said (in some other part of the constituent) not to exist in that world. So the negation of such a constituent is a logical truth. Looking for inconsistent constituents is of interest since if a constituent is inconsistent that means the world cannot have the types of objects occurring in the constituent conjunctively (at the same time). That, however, means that the presence of some type of individual excludes some other type of individual. This can be expressed by a logical truth (a conditional). If the antecedent of this logical truth is of a depth smaller than that of the consequent we have discovered an information increasing logical truth.

So at the level of basic predicates we have conjunctions like:

(21) $P_1(x) \land P_2(x) \land \neg P_3(x)...$

each giving us a Q-predicate $Q_1(x)$, $Q_2(x)$.

At the level of constituents we have:

(22) $(\exists x)Q_1(x) \land \neg(\neg \exists x)Q_2(x)$

Allowing for basic relations in Q_i means that within a Q-predicate '$\forall$' can occur (i.e. a nesting '$\exists x \forall y$'), since referring to another individual is done (at least in part) with definite descriptions

(23) $(\exists x)(\forall y)(...x... \supset x=y)$

Checking for consistency is done depth by depth, looking for trivial inconsistency at the subordinate clauses' depth (the subordinate clauses being the ones within the scope of another quantifier) by instantiating the variables bound by '$\exists$'. Like constituents, logical truths get assigned a corresponding depth in the procedure. If you formulate these logical truths as conditionals you see which of them are information increasing.

This procedure is, of course (since First Order Logic is not decidable), not effective when applied to the non-finite case – which makes so checking the applicability of closure under K non-effective. Given that we know A being a logical truth counting its quantificational depth is effective. So determining the logical truth of a formula should be distinguished from determining whether it has an information increasing structure.

What can we say about Hintikka's approach then? There seem to be quite a few open questions:

- Is this a psychological theory? Where from? It seems nobody employs these procedures or the corresponding measures. So let us assume it is a model for some unspecified process going on in assessing and recognising logical truths. The model may explain why information is gained by consequences, but it does not say which information we get if it were to be expressed in words.

- Why are just quantifiers the problem? Even though PC is decidable we might not be able to discover that some A is a tautology. So even closure within propositional epistemic logic is a problem.

- Why not simply say we do not know all the consequences of our beliefs, since this surpasses our capacities because of computational complexity (we have not enough time and storage) or – in some cases – undecidability?

Although Hintikka employs the machinery of the semantic approach the procedure looks cumbersome and non-effective.

That might be reasons to look for another approach (within situation semantics or some version of a syntactic approach).

Algorithmic Information Theory to the Rescue?

Algorithmic Information Theory (see Chapter 1|3) is a theory of informational content, not of information flow. It deals with word strings. The basic measure is the same like in the original syntactic approach: bits. But Algorithmic Information Theory focuses not simply on the coding scheme but on matters of generating a word string by a program. A string has some measure in bits. The informational content of a string is the length of the shortest program (in bits) which is needed to generate the string. The length of the shortest program for a string is also its complexity. A finite string of length n can be 'programmed' by having it simply printed, with length n+k, k being the length in bits of the minimal code to print it. (The real problem is infinite strings, but since there are no infinite sentences this is no problem here.) A string is random if the size of the shortest program for it, if there is any, is not shorter than the string itself. Most strings are random, since there are more strings than well-formed programs. So the great majority of strings of length n are of complexity very close to n. So the basic definitions of interest here are (Definition 1|3–1 and Definition 1|3–2 from Chapter 1|3): The complexity $I_c(s)$ of a binary string s is defined to be the length of the shortest program p that makes the computer C output s, i.e. $I_c(s) = \min\;[\lg(p)|\;C(p)=s]$; a random binary string s is one having the property that $I(s) \approx \lg(s)$. The complexity $I_c(s)$ mentioned here defines also the informational content of a string. If you know its complexity you know the amount of information present in it.

Algorithmic Information Theory could be a syntactic solution at least to the problem why different logical truths have different informational content. Logical truths – at least those which are theorems within a logical system – are not random one would expect, since by their very definition there are programs for them: one could assume that one program capable to generate a string that is a logical truth is its proof! So logical truth would have definite informational content, and different logical truths could have different ones. (Given that we single out that program.) And given that we have found the shortest proofs of them we have the length of the proof available, so that we can see whether much or not so much information is gained in a logic course.

The problem with this approach is that we almost never have an effective procedure to find the shortest proof of a formula, even if we know that it is a logical truth. For that reason an approach like one based on intensional isomorphy may be favoured.

Further Reading

Look for the chapters mentioned for the details of the approaches mentioned. Hintikka developed his approach in his classical paper

- 'Surface Information and Depth Information', in: Jaakko Hintikka/Patrick Suppes (eds.), *Information and Inference*, Dordrecht 1970.

See also the papers in his collection:

- *Logic, Language-Games and Information*, Oxford 1973.

and

- Veikko Rantala, 'Urn Models. A New Kind of Non-Standard Model for First-Order Logic', *Journal of Philosophical Logic* 4 (1975), 455-474.

3 | The Causal Approach to Information
The Information You Have But Do Not Believe

ON a warm and sunny day, somewhere in the middle of East Africa, a young hominide stares blinking up in the sky, using his hand as a sun-shield. It is about Noon, some 5 million years ago, on a Wednesday. What caught the attention of our young friend is a couple of (what we would call) vultures who are flying in little circles above an area which is about 3 kilometers away.

It is not the beauty of their elegant hovering in the air that is of interest for the hominide, but whatever is the cause of their hovering over the savannah. It will be a wounded animal that could turn this lousy Wednesday into a Sunday. The hominide jumps up – albuminous nourishment – a good day to develop bipedalism...

An old but still rather well-known creation myth starts with the phrase 'In the beginning there was the word'. Well, as we know today, words weren't there from the beginning. In fact, it was only somewhere between 2 million and 100000 years ago that *homo* developed a phonetic language on Earth (alas we do not know of other planets where life and language might have evolved earlier, but definitely nowhere was it there 'from the beginning'). But before that, the now extinct *hominides* in Africa have nevertheless been able to exploit a good that we nowadays see in a very intimate connection with words; they were able to exploit *information*.

In the story above it is the information that a wounded animal is about 3 km away, pretty close to where the vultures are flying their little circles. Their flights did carry this information. It was out there, ready for the hominide to pick it up and to exploit it for his purposes.

This is a view on information which is somewhat at odds with the philosophical tradition. How can information just be there? Even without a perceiver? Without a mind who categorizes the world and has interests relative to which and in virtue of which things can carry information.

Of course, some traditional philosophers had even a hard time to accept that mountains, trees and the moon could exist independent of anyone watching them, so the worries of philosophers concerning mind independent *information* should maybe not bother us. But shouldn't it then also be possible to have information but not believing it? And is not information intertwined with knowledge and knowledge with belief? How can all that be systematized and still remain in the least plausible?

3|1   The Causal Theory of Information Flow

> Information [...] is an objective commodity, the sort of thing that can be delivered to, processed by, and transmitted from instruments, gauges, computers, and neurons. It is something that can be *in* the optic array, on the printed page, carried by a temporal configuration of electrical pulses, and stored on a magnetic disk, and it exists there *whether or not anyone appreciates this fact or knows how to extract it*. It is something that was in this world before we got here. It was, I submit, the raw material out of which minds were manufactured. (Dretske 1983, 223)

Information is out there
As becomes clear from this quote, Dretske understands information as a phenomenon of the world, which exists independently of its actual or potential use by any interpreter. The counterintuitiveness of this view to some is in Dretske's words due to a 'confusion of information with meaning'. Getting clear about the difference between meaning and information, will enable us to think about information as an objective commodity, something the generation, transmission, and reception of which does not require or in any way presuppose interpretive processes.

Back to MCT
Dretske bases his account on what was achieved by MCT already. As we've learned in chapter 1|2, MCT identifies the amount of information associated with, or generated by, the occurrence of an event with the reduction of uncertainty, the elimination of possibilities, represented by that state of affairs. When an ensemble of possibilities is thus reduced, the amount of information associated with the result is a function of how many possibilities were eliminated in reaching that result.

Amount vs. Content
MCT gives us a general formula for computing the amount of information generated by the reduction of *n* possibilities to 1. If s (the source) is some mechanism or process the result of which is the reduc-

tion of *n* equally likely possibilities to 1, and we write 'I(s)' to denote the amount of information associated, or generated by, s, then

$$I(s) = \log n.$$

This will give us the amount of information every signal informing us about s will carry. But it will not give us the informational *content* of any message, it doesn't discriminate messages in this way.

Average Amount

How we can go on to find a formula for a source producing non-equiprobable results, and how we can determine how much of the information generated at the source is received after transmission, should by now be clear, but we shall briefly recapitulate the most important points. (But will use Dretske's notation. We think it will then be easier for you to find the things in Dretske's book if you want to look things up one day. You will be familiar with everything anyway, if you note that $H(A)$, the entropy of a finite scheme is here I(s), the average amount of information produced at a source, and $I(s_j) = 1/p(s_j)$.)

The formula for computing the *average* amount of information associated with a given source s, I(s) in short, is

Entropy of s
$I(s) = \Sigma p(s_j) \times I(s_j)$

MCT, being concerned with engineering problems, deals with the average amount of information produced and transmitted. To set up a communication system it matters most that the system works for the things it is most likely to do. But this will not be of much importance to us, for we are now interested in the informational content carried by *specific* signals rather than with the amount of information produced and transmitted on average.

Noise and Equivocation

We remember that noise can reduce the information received. I(s) is the amount of information generated at the source, I(r) the amount of information generated at the receiver, then $I_s(r)$ is the amount of information received about s at r:

$$I_s(r) = I(r) - \text{noise}$$

$$I_s(r) = I(s) - \text{equivocation}$$

Whereas equivocation is the information lost in the communication process, and noise that information added to the transmitted message that is not about s.

The equivocation a specific received signal carries, say r_7, is computed by selecting the various events that might occur at the receiver r, say $r_1...r_8$, and calculating their individual *contributions* to the average equivocation (we have done all that at the end of chapter 1|2, but repeat it here in Dretske's notation, $P(s_j|r_7)$ being the conditional probability for s_j given r_7.):

> **Definition 3|1–1**
>
> $E(r_7) = -\Sigma P(s_j|r_7) \times \log P(s_j|r_7)$

The equivocation considers the likelihood that s_j was sent/intended when r_7 is received. The contribution of a certain state, s_7, at the source s to the noise is calculated accordingly:

> **Definition 3|1–2**
>
> $N(s_7) = -\Sigma P(r_j|s_7) \times \log P(r_j|s_7)$

The noise considers the likelihood that r_j is received given that s_7 is sent. These Definitions enable us to compute the equivocation and the noise associated with a specific instance of communication, rather than the noise and equivocation associated with a source and a receiver on average.

Causation and Information

If a theory of information treats information as an objective commodity of our world, independent of minds and interpreting agents, a causal story seems to suggest itself. Smoke means fire, because fire causes smoke. It seems, as the transmission of information has been described, it is a process that depends on the causal interrelatedness of source and receiver. The way one gets a message from s to r is by initiating a sequence of events at s that culminates in a corresponding sequence at r. In abstract terms, 'the message is borne from s and r by a causal process which determines what happens at r in terms of what happens at s' (Dretske 1981, 26). Thus information flow should crucially reduce to something like this (the arrow indicating a causal connection)

This view is correct insofar as the flow of information may and in most cases does depend on underlying causal processes, however, the informational relationships between s and r must be distinguished from the total system of causal relationships existing between these points. Causation is certainly not sufficient for information to flow, since different s-states can cause the same r-state. Consider the situations 2 and 3 from figure 3|1–1: In both situations the solid arrow represents an actually obtaining causal connection between the source event s and the receiver event r. The dotted lines indicate counterfactual causal dependencies that do not actually obtain. Thus, if in situation 1, s_1 happened, r_1 would be caused, etc.

In situation 1 the different r events are causally connected with distinct s events. The equivocation of the signal r_2 in situation 1 is zero,

THE CAUSAL THEORY OF INFORMATION FLOW

since s_2 is the *only* source event that causes r_2. We can plug this into definition 1:

$$\begin{aligned}E(r_2) = -[&P(s_2|r_2) \times \log P(s_2|r_2) + \\ &P(s_1|r_2) \times \log P(s_1|r_2) + \\ &P(s_3|r_2) \times \log P(s_3|r_2) + \\ &P(s_4|r_2) \times \log P(s_4|r_2)]\end{aligned}$$

The first term $[P(s_2|r_2) \times \log P(s_2|r_2)]$ will be zero, since the probability

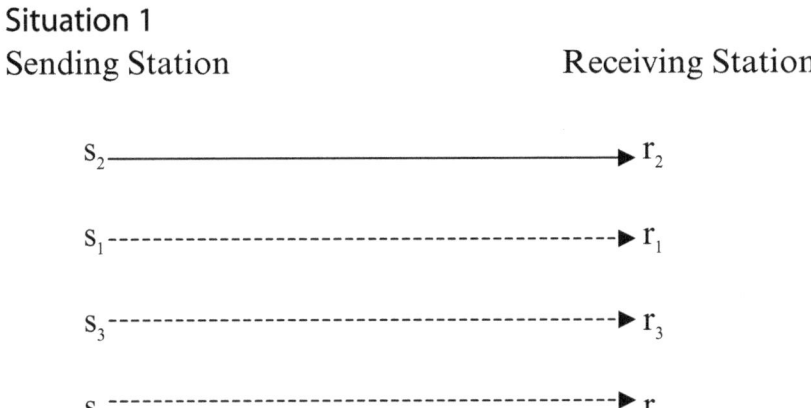

Figure 3|1-1

for s_2, given r_2 is unity and the logarithm of 1 is 0. All other terms beneath will be zero for the conditional probability of s_i (with $i \neq 2$) given r_2 is zero. Assuming that the source events are all equally likely, a full 2 bits of information from s gets through.

Now, consider situation 2. Again s_2 occurs at the source and brings about r_2 at the receiver. Nevertheless, the amount of information transmitted is entirely different. Let's calculate the equivocation of r_2:

$$\begin{aligned} E(r_2) = &-[\, P(s_2|r_2) \times \log P(s_2|r_2) + &-[1/3 \times \log 1|3 + \\ & P(s_1|r_2) \times \log P(s_1|r_2) + & 1/3 \times \log 1/3 + \\ & P(s_3|r_2) \times \log P(s_3|r_2) + & 1/3 \times \log 1/3 + \\ & P(s_4|r_2) \times \log P(s_4|r_2)\,] & 0\,] \approx 1.6 \text{ bits} \end{aligned}$$

The logarithm of 1/3 is approximately -1.6, thus the equivocation of r_2 is approximately 1.6 bits. Therefore r_2 carries only .4 bits of information about s (2 bits of information were generated at s). In terms of what actually happens and which causal connections actually obtain, situation 1 and 2 cannot be distinguished. Thus the causal story alone (that s_2 brought about r_2) cannot tell us how much information is transmitted. The obtaining of a causal connection between source and receiver is obviously not a sufficient condition for information flow.

From the second situation we can also learn a further lesson. If we concentrate on s_4 in situation 2, we see that s_4 at the source might bring about any of the remaining r-states. Let's assume that by chance the obtaining of s_4 will cause r_1 to occur in 34 percent of the time, and r_3 and r_4 in 33 percent of the time, respectively. Now, if s_4 should occur in the communication system depicted in situation 2, any of the events at r (r_1, r_3, r_4) will carry a full 2 bits of information about the source. In contrast to r_2, the remaining r-states will tell us definitely what happened at s. Although these r-states are less predictable given what state s is in than r_2, they carry more information. In short: the transmission of information between source and receiver does not depend on the presence of a deterministic process connecting them. Moreover, Dretske argues that the obtaining of a causal connection between source

Situation 3

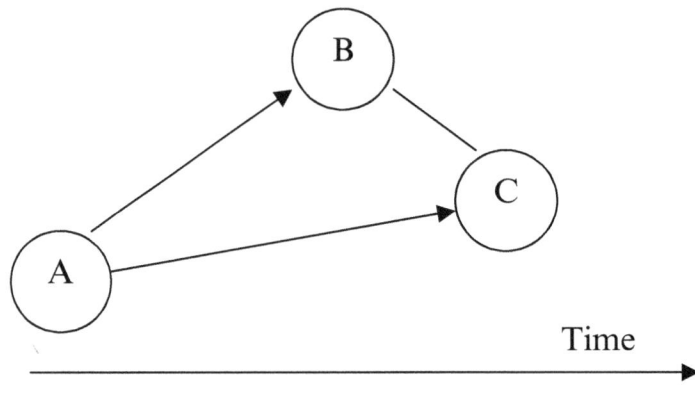

Figure 3|1–2

and receiver isn't even necessary for information to flow. Consider situation 3 in Figure 3|1–2.

A is causally connected with B and C, but there is no causal connection between B and C. Think of A as being the TV station in your vicinity, B your TV set and C the TV set of Pavel Pippowicz, a Czech TV junky who lives on the other side of the planet with a TV set that receives only one channel (the one broadcasted by the TV station in your hometown). Form looking at your TV screen you learn what Pavel is looking at. There is an information channel between B and C, although what happens on your TV screen is not caused by what happens at Pavel's TV screen. There is a 'ghost channel' connecting the source and the receiver, but information gets through.

We can put this even stronger. Assume that Pavel receives the program of your hometown's TV station with a delay of 30 second in relation to your TV due to the way the signal from A to C has to travel. Now you know what happens at Pavel's TV already 30 seconds before it is going to happen. If we assume that there is no backwards causation, i.e. that a cause has always to precede (and might, at best, be simultaneous with) its effect in the temporal order of things, there cannot be a causal relation between source (C) and receiver (B) in principle. Nevertheless, information flows. (We should add that some philosophers think that there is backwards causation. See Phil Dowe's work on causal loops, for example (Dowe manuscript). But the first argument would, of course, still hold.)

Going Further

MCT does not tell us what information is. It ignores, as we have seen already, all questions having to do with the content of signals, what specific information they carry, in order to describe how much information they carry. But in doing so it is still interesting for our aim to understand what information is. Since by analyzing how much information a signal carries, MCT *imposes constraints on what information a signal can carry*, constraints we can use to develop an account of how much information a signal does carry. Consider the following analogy from Dretske: we can clearly distinguish a signal from its content. Two short knocks is the signal, that the courier has arrived is the message. We can also distinguish a bucket from what it contains. This is why MCT does not tell us directly what information is.

Nevertheless, learning that a bucket can contain only 1 liter of any given liquid might inform us about what liquid the bucket carries, for it might be the case that the bucket will either carry one liter of beer or 2 liters of lemonade. Given that we know of the one liter constraint, we prefer one of the hypotheses concerning the content. Accordingly: given the constraints set up by MCT we may prefer some fitting theory of informational content. This is the way in which MCT is still important for a theory of information.

Although Dretske goes on to analyze information as a semantic concept, he warns us not to confuse information with meaning. Not every meaningful message carries information and even if it carries information, this information doesn't have to be identical with its meaning.

'I am drunk.' is meaningful, independent of its truth. But this sentence carries information only if what this sentence asserts is true.

> What information a signal carries is what it is capable of 'telling' us, telling us truly, about another state of affairs. Roughly speaking, information is

that commodity of yielding knowledge, and what information a signal carries is what we can learn from it. (Dretske 1981, 44)

'False information' or 'misinformation' are not kinds of information, according to this view. 'Reliable Information' is a redundant way of speaking. Additionally, 'I am drunk' means that the speaker is drunk, not that the speaker is drunk or lives on the moon. But the signal 'I am drunk' carries the information that the speaker is drunk or is on the moon, if it carries the information that the speaker is drunk.

The information a signal carries might therefore well exceed its meaning. Consider the following case: You know that the only alcohol Simon possibly drinks (if ever) is *Pilsener Urquell*. Hearing him utter 'I am drunk.' you get the information that Simon must have been drinking *Pilsener Urquell* (in fact, too much of it). That the signal, viz. Simon's utterance, carries this information is not part of the meaning of his utterance. Even events with no conventional meaning at all might carry information; remember that smoke carries the information that there is fire. Therefore information is not meaning. The interesting question is not whether or not MCT is a theory of meaning or might support a theory of meaning; the question is whether it will help us with a theory of *information*.

How we can exploit MCT

As we have said already, MCT is interested in the average amount of information. The information produced by a particular event or the information carried by a particular signal about a source were not formulas of MCT, they were at best intermediate steps on the way to the formulas of MCT dealing with the average amounts. The formulas for the amount of information generated by a particular source (given non-equiprobable possibilities) and the formula for the information carried by a particular signal about some source, should by now be obvious:

Definition 3|1–3
The amount of information generated by a particular event $s_a =_{df}$ $I(s_a) = \log 1/p(s_a)$

Definition 3|1–4
The amount of information carried by a particular signal r_a about s_a $=_{df} Is(r_a) = I(s_a) - E(r_a)$

whereas $E(r_a)$ is understood to be the equivocation associated with the particular signal r_a.

To apply definition 3|1–3 and 3|1–4 to concrete situations seems to involve an estimate of the alternative possibilities. But what are the alternative possibilities to my ... cruising with my skateboard?, playing guitar?, eating lunch?, ... What are the associated probabilities of all these possibilities? What are the conditional possibilities of each of these given the configuration of photons reaching your visual receptors from a tv-screen showing me skateboarding? We should know all these if we want an absolute measure, a definite numerical figure for the amount of information generated by an event or carried by a signal.

Although we cannot get such an absolute measure, we can use these formulas to make comparisons, in particular comparisons between the amount of information generated by the occurrence of an event and the amount of information a signal carries about that event.

For informational content we want to know, not how much information is generated by the occurrence of s_a, not how much information r_a carries about the occurrence of this event, but whether r_a carries as much information about s_a as is generated by its occurrence. In order to answer this question, one does not have to know the value of $I(s_a)$ or the value of $I_s(r_a)$. Inspection of

$$Is(r_a) = I(s_a) - E(r_a)$$

shows that all one has to know is whether the equivocation is zero or not. In this case the signal carries as much information as is generated at the source.

The Xerox Principle

Given these considerations, we can formulate the famous Xerox-Principle:

> **Definition 3|1–5 (Xerox Principle)**
>
> If *A* carries the information that *B*, and *B* carries the information that *C*, then *A* carries the information that *C*.

This principle is indeed fundamental for any theory of information flow. For information to flow it presupposes that the equivocation will be zero.

A Semantical Theory of Information

Given these consideration we can now state two conditions, information must satisfy:

If a signal carries the information that s is F, it must be the case that

(A) The signal carries as much information about s as would be generated by s's being F.

Furthermore, if a signal carries the information that s is F, it must be the case that

(B) s is F.

(A) and (B) are both necessary but still not jointly sufficient. Suppose s is a red square. Suppose further that s's being red generates 3 bits of information and so does s's being square. Now a signal carrying the information that s is square carries as much information as is generated by s's being red and s is red, but the signal doesn't carry this information.

(C) The quantity of information the signal carries about s is (or includes) that quantity generated by s's being F (and not, say, by s's being G).

(A) is the *communication condition*, (B) and (C) are the *semantic conditions* on information.

Now we are in a position to formulate a definition of the information contained in a signal that simultaneously satisfies these three conditions.

> **Definition 3|1–6 (Informational Content)**
>
> A signal r carries the information that s is F = The conditional probability of s's being F, given r (and k), is 1 (but given k alone, less than 1).

Whereas k stands for what the receiver already knows about the possibilities that exist at the source.

It makes little sense to speak of *the* informational content a signal carries. For if a signal carries the information that s is F, and s's being F carries the information that s is G, then this same signal carries the information that s is G.

In general, if there is a natural law to the effect that whenever s is F, t is G, then no signal can bear the message that s is F without also conveying the information that t is G. We can account for this nested in information by the following definition:

> **Definition 3|1–7 (Nested Information)**
>
> The information that t is G is nested in s's being F = s's being F carries the information that t is G.

Such nesting can be *analytical* or *nomical*. This feature of information will help again to distinguish the concept of information sharply from meaning. 'Joe is at home or at the office' is not part of the meaning of 'Joe is at home' but if a statement carries the information that Joe is at home, it thereby carries the information that Joe is either at home or at the office.

Further Reading
The entire chapter is based on

- Fred Dretske, *Knowledge and the Flow of Information*, Cambridge/Mass. (MIT Press) 1981.

A brief summary is given in

- Fred Dretske, 'Précis of Knowledge and the Flow of Information', *Behavioral and Brain Sciences* 6 (1983), 55-63.

For a critical discussion of Dretske's view, as presented in *Knowledge and the Flow of Information*, you can find a lot in a Synthese volume that is dedicated to information theoretic epistemology and semantics:

- Barry Loewer (ed.), 'Information Theoretic Epistemology and Semantics', *Synthese* 70 (No. 2, February 1987), 157-317.

3|2 Information in Externalist Epistemology

The JTB-theory of Knowledge

Philosophers have for a long time thought that knowledge could be analyzed as being justified true belief. That is, if anyone or anything could be said to have the knowledge that p, the subject in question must have the belief that p, p must be the case and the subject should be justified in believing that p. Here is an example:

Consider that I claim that somebody is standing outside the door. For my claim to knowledge to be true, I first of all have to *believe* that somebody is standing outside the door. For example if I told a lie with my utterance 'Somebody is standing outside the door', I would not believe it myself that it is true what I say. This could not count as knowledge, even if it were in fact true by incidence that somebody *is* standing outside the door (thus even if I said, by incidence, something true with my utterance).

In addition to that, it must be true what I believe. If I believe that somebody is standing outside the door, but in fact there is no one, my belief does not count as knowledge. To believe a proposition is a necessary condition for knowing the proposition, but not sufficient for knowing it. Thus for my belief to count as *knowledge*, somebody must really be standing outside the door; it must be true, what I believe.

Now, imagine that I'm a nervous guy. I watched a horror movie at the cinemas and now back at home am still quite exhilarated. Lying in bed that evening, I can hardly sleep, believing all the time that some monster, murderer, or alien is standing behind the curtain, lying under my bed or hiding in the closet. In the course of this paranoia, I also come to believe (without having any evidence for it) that somebody is standing outside the door. By incidence, there is in fact somebody standing outside the door. It is Manuel, who came to visit me and chop me up because this chapter is way over deadline. Now I believe that somebody is standing outside the door and, in addition, this belief is true. But would that count as knowledge?

Well, irrational people would probably say that my belief was knowledge. Because of my paranoia I acquired something like a sixth sense which accounts for my knowledge that somebody was standing outside the door, I did mysteriously presage it, a case of clairvoyance. Although I erred about the alien under the bed, the monster in the closet and the murderer behind the curtain, I was right about the butcher behind the door, and that was knowledge.

Most philosophers, on the other hand, do not share this intuition. For them my belief was just a guess, a hunch or inkling, but it was not knowledge. I had no reason to belief that somebody was standing outside the door, I had heard no noises and had no appointment made with Manuel so that I could assume him to be outside the door that time. Although I had a belief which was incidentally true, I could not know that Manuel was ambuscading me behind the door.

Therefore most philosophers thought that knowledge must be more than mere true belief. In addition, the belief must be justified. I must have reasons for my belief that show that it isn't a mere hunch what I believe. It's only then that what I believe could count as knowledge. This is what is the standard account of knowledge (put forward already by Plato):

> **Definition 3|2–1 (JTB-Theory of Knowledge)**
>
> A subject s knows that p iff
> (i) s believes that p,
> (ii) p is true,
> (iii) s can justify his belief that

What is expressed in Definition 3|2–1 is what we will call *the justified-belief-theory of knowledge*, or the 'JTB-theory of Knowledge' for short.

Is the JTB-theory of Knowledge False?

In 1963 Paul Gettier attacked the JTB-theory of Knowledge with two counterexamples which spun off a number of attacks in the same vein. That is what gave the name for these kind of thought experiments, the so-called 'Gettier-cases'. Gettier's own counterexamples are not necessarily convincing, which is why we will present a modified thought experiment.

Imagine that Gerard visits for the first time his good friend Louis in his house in Versailles, France. Louis and Gerard both share an awkward interest in the 17th century, which is why they both dress up like 17th century French kings when they meet. Having arrived in Versailles, Gerard enters the house of his good friend Louis, let in by Louis' manservant. As he enters the somewhat gloomy hall, he spots another person coming towards him, wearing a wig and an odd looking garment just like him, and Gerard comes to believe that Louis is standing about 30ft. from him.

Louis is in fact standing exactly 30ft. in front of Gerard but, unbeknownst to Gerard, Louis is standing behind a wall that Gerard is walking towards to. At Gerard's side of the wall hangs a huge mirror reflecting Gerard's own funny appearance back to himself, which is what he mistook for being the approaching Louis. (We can assume that on Louis' side of the wall is a mirror as well and that Louis is brushing up his make-up again, if you wonder why Louis should be standing behind a wall.)

This seems to be a case in which Gerard has a true belief, viz. that Louis is standing about 30ft. in front of him, which is, moreover, a justified belief: Gerard perceives the shape of a person which looks just like Louis quite often looks, Gerard is in Louis' own house, and he has an appointment with Louis at that time, all pretty good reasons to believe that it is Louis who is standing 30ft. in front of him. But although this justifies Gerard's belief, we would not say that Gerard *knows* that Louis is standing 30ft. in front of him. The perceiving which justifies his belief is in fact not informing him of the whereabouts of Louis. It is his own reflection that he mistakes for Louis.

Being a justified, true belief thus seems not to be enough for knowledge. Philosophers have then tried to find additional constraints, constraints for justification, which could rule out beliefs like Gerard's as being justified. However, this enterprise isn't that convincing to some, since if justification is something that you demand from the epistemic subject, then your demands should not overstrain the abilities of this subject. But what else could Gerard possibly have done more to justify his belief that Louis is standing 30ft. in front of him?

Dretske's New Approach

Dretske's information-theoretic account of knowledge tries to do without notions like justification, evidence, or certainty altogether. Since Dretske is convinced that the Gettier cases have made obvious the shortcomings of the JTB-theory, an epistemology must be developed which does not rely on these concepts.

To develop such a 'naturalized' epistemology is certainly an ambitious project. The idea is, in Dretske's words, 'to bake a mental cake using only physical yeast and flour' (Dretske 1981, xi). Thus it is pardonable that Dretske limits his project to only one sort of knowledge, so-called 'de re perceptual knowledge'. This is the knowledge involved if a epistemic subject perceptually knows of some a that it is F.

To clarify this notion somewhat, imagine that you are walking down Beverly Hills on a shopping tour and in front of you walks Edward Van Halen. You do not recognize him as being Eddie Van Halen, but notice by looking at the person walking in front of you that this guy has quite long dark hair. You thereby come perceptually to know of Eddie Van Halen that he has long dark hair.

But, nevertheless, you might not *de dicto* know that Eddie Van Halen has dark hair. You might have failed to notice that you were walking behind Eddie Van Halen and might have been raised without being exposed to MTV. Thus if somebody asks you of which color the hair of Eddie Van Halen is you might not be able to answer correctly. Nevertheless you know *de re* of Eddie Van Halen that he has dark hair, for it was Eddie Van Halen who walked down Beverly Hills in front of you and you know from seeing it that the person in front of you has dark hair.

The limitation to perceptual knowledge is simply the limitation to knowledge we can achieve by looking at things, touching, smelling, or hearing them. There might be other ways of coming to know of something, for example ways of coming to know of abstract objects and their properties which might not be reducible to perception, but this we also will blend out, following Dretske.

Now, Dretske argues for an analysis of knowledge which is based on the information theory he developed subsequent to Shannon and Weaver. The basic analysis is the following equation:

> **Definition 3|2–2**
>
> An epistemic subject s knows that a is F = s's belief that a is F is caused (or causally sustained) by the information that a is F.

From the preceding chapter we remember what conditions must hold for a signal to carry the information that a is F:

(A) The signal carries as much information about *a* as would be generated by *a*'s being F.

(B) *a* is *F*.

(C) The quantity of information the signal carries about *a* is (or includes) that quantity generated by *a*'s being *F* (and not, say, by *a*'s being *G*).

We halve also learned that Dretske takes the following Definition of informational content to satisfy these conditions:

> **Definition 3|2–3**
>
> *Informational content*: A signal r carries the information that a is F = The conditional probability of a's being F, given r (and k), is 1 (but given k alone, less than 1).

We remember that k was the abbreviation for the background knowledge the epistemic subject already has about the source. One could wonder if this doesn't render Dretske's analysis viciously circular. If knowledge is analyzed on the right hand side of Definition 3|2–2 with recourse to the information that caused a belief, and information is analyzed in Definition 3|2–3 with recourse to what the epistemic subject already *knows* about the source, one could worry that this covert reference to knowledge in the right hand side of Definition 3|2–2 keeps the definition from telling us what knowledge is. We have to know already what knowledge is to even apply the definition.

Dretske argues that this is only an apparent vicious circularity. In fact his definition is intended to have a recursive character, which saves the definition from becoming viciously circular.

Note that whether an epistemic subject learns that *a* is *F* may depend on what *else* he knows about the source, but it is not said to depend on his already knowing that *a* is *F*. Thus the definition is at least not blatantly circular in that it would simply translate into

> Definition 3|2-4
>
> ---
>
> s knows that a is F = s knows that a is F.

But still Definition 3|2-2 is circular, for the right hand side makes covert reference to the definiendum, viz. to knowledge. But not every circularity is a vicious one. Definitions which are recursive might be circular, but are not viciously so, if the recursive application of the definition will in all cases terminate. To get clear on this rather important point, we shall look at an example:

Consider a three-cards monte game. Exactly one ace of shades is known to be among the three cards on the table. You have already investigated the leftmost of the cards and found it not to be the ace of shades. Given what you know, there are only two possibilities left. When you turn the middle card over and find that it, as well, isn't the ace of shades, this observation carries the information that the ace of shades is the rightmost card. The observation carries this information, because of what you already *know* about the cards. If we are interested in whether you really know that the leftmost card isn't the ace of shades, we can simply reapply our definition to this different piece of knowledge. When you turned over the leftmost card and observed the front of the card, did this observation really carry the information that the leftmost card isn't the ace of shades? If the observation did carry the information that the leftmost card isn't the ace of shade and if this information caused or causally sustained your belief that the leftmost card isn't the ace of shades, then you know that the leftmost card isn't the ace of shades. If this piece of information did, again, depend on any background knowledge about the source, we can continue reapplying our formula to this collateral knowledge. This recursive application terminates when we eventually reach the point where the information you received does not depend on any prior knowledge about the source. The fact that the recursive application will eventually terminate enables Dretske's definition to avoid circularity.

What Beliefs are and How They Can be Caused by Information

But how does something as abstract as information cause anything – and beliefs in particular? Let's first see how information could cause anything.

Suppose that a spy is waiting for a courier to arrive and they agreed on the secret sign that the courier will knock three times quickly at the door, followed by a pause and another three quick knocks. This sequence of knocks then carries the information that the courier has arrived. The signal r (the sequence of knocks) carries the information that s is F (that the courier has arrived) in virtue of r's being F' (the sequence of knocks having a certain temporal pattern, but not in virtue of having a certain pitch or in virtue of occurring at a certain time of the day).

When a signal r (the sequence of knocks) carries the information that s is F (that the courier arrived) in virtue of having the property F' (this temporal pattern), then and only then does the information that s is F (that the courier arrived) cause simply whatever the signal's being F' causes.

Beliefs, on the other hand, are tokens of representational types, tokens of structures that can represent or misrepresent how things stand. In a way, beliefs are what Dretske calls tokens of 'semantic structures', they are interpretations of the incoming and information-bearing signals of the system. These tokens can be *triggered* by signals that carry information. Beliefs can also be triggered by other beliefs in the internal proceedings of some informational system. If a signal that carries the information that *a* is *F* causes by virtue of being *F'* a token of the structure which is selectively sensitive to the *F*-ness of things to occur, information will *produce* knowledge.

Counterexamples to Dretske's Analysis of Knowledge

As nothing remains undisputed in philosophy, some philosophers have developed thought experiments to falsify Dretske's theory of knowledge. We shall discuss three of them in turn, to see how Dretske's theory works. As it turns out all of them seem to fail for very similar reasons, which will help us to understand Dretske's theory a little better as well. Let's first look at the three little stories:

> (i) A machine is equipped with a red indicator light which shines iff the machine becomes too hot. K walks by the machine and observes that the red light shines, but doesn't know what that means. He asks H, who is usually reliable and whom K trusts. H doesn't know either what the red light is good for, but announces with the voice of authority that the red light means that the machine is too hot. K comes to believe that the machine is too hot. Is this knowledge? Intuition says no.

> (ii) S visits a marvelous planetarium which is in fact so good that one thinks one would directly look at the evening sky. In parts of the ceiling of the planetarium are windows through which one can actually see the evening sky and it is difficult to tell the difference of whether one is looking at the ceiling or looking through one of the windows at the actual sky. S falls asleep in the planetarium, wakes up after a while without recollection of where he is. He sees a star through one of the windows and forms the belief that he's looking at a star. Is this knowledge? Intuition says no.

> (iii) Again, eight employees must be reduced to one. H is the one selected. The employees have chosen to inform the boss not via the written word, but via the color of the envelope passed to the boss. Each employee was assigned a color before the selection process, H was assigned pink. Thus a pink envelope is passed to the boss. Holding the envelope in his hands, the boss forms the belief that H is the one selected, not because the boss would know of the convention adopted by his employees, this he doesn't know, but because of the fact that the pink color of the envelope reminds him of H's hideous pink

ties (which, on the other hand played absolutely no role in the assignment of colors among the employees). Is this knowledge? Intuition says no.

Of course, all purported counterexamples assume that Dretske's theory would in all cases have to say that it was knowledge and thus be in conflict with our intuitions. In fact Dretske's theory does not say that.

Consider case (i). K comes to believe that the machine is too hot. This belief is obviously true, but is it knowledge? Well, K's believe is caused by listening to H's explanation and the observation of the red light. Was it *information* about the source that caused the belief that the machine is too hot? The only signal that could have carried the information that the machine is too hot is the red light. Did K's observation of the red light carry the information that the machine is too hot?

Alone it obviously didn't. The observation of the red light did not reduce the conditional probability of the machine being too hot to 1, given what else K knew about the machine. He didn't know what the red light indicated, that's why he asked H for help. What H said didn't carry the information that the machine is too hot either. In fact it didn't carry any information (for H made it all up and only got it right by incident). Thus the belief of K, that the red light indicates that the machine is too hot, which was caused by what H said, was not caused by information and thus doesn't count as knowledge. Therefore, K doesn't know that the machine is too hot.

Consider case (ii). This one is related, but a bit trickier. There are relevant alternatives that S overlooks when he comes to believe that he is looking at a star, viz. the relevant alternative that he is in fact mistaking a simulated point of light from the planetarium projector for a star. S overlooks this relevant alternative, because he has forgotten that he actually is in a planetarium. That he is not looking at an oncoming train in a tunnel or a simulated point of light at the ceiling of a marvelous planetarium is his background belief that was probably caused by his observation that the surrounding area he is looking at is dark and somehow above him and resembles the night sky. However, these background beliefs of S which excluded possibilities for him as apparently irrelevant do not count as *knowledge*. They are not caused or sustained by the information that what S is looking at is the plain night sky, for S is not looking at the plain night sky. S is looking through a window of a marvelous planetarium which he mistakes to be the night sky. Thus the possibilities S excluded were not excluded by knowledge. Therefore the observation that he makes of the star does not carry the information for S that it is a star S is looking at. Again, the signal doesn't raise the conditional probability of a's being F, given r (and k), to 1, the signal doesn't have the informational content needed to produce knowledge.

Consider case (iii). This one seems to be the trickiest. Above we said that when a signal r carries the information that s is F in virtue of having the property F', then and only then does the information that s is F cause simply whatever the signal's being F' causes. The boss believes that the employee who was selected is H. This belief is caused by the pinkness of the envelope. Now, when a signal r (the envelope) carries the information that s is F (that H was selected) in virtue of having the property F' (being pink), then and only then does the information that s is F (that H was selected) cause simply whatever the signal's being F' causes. The signal's being F' is what causes the belief of the boss, thus it should be knowledge, shouldn't it?

Again, this objection overlooks that if the receiver has to rely on background beliefs to get at the information carried by r, it is of crucial importance to see whether or not these beliefs qualify as knowledge. This is constitutive for the *informational content* the signal has. To find out whether the boss' background beliefs were knowledge is done by reapplying Definition 3|2–2, that's the recursive character of Dretske's theory of knowledge. The signal in our example doesn't have the informational content that a is F (that H was selected) alone since the signal as such doesn't raise the conditional probability for a's being F given r and k to 1. In fact, the informational content of r, given k, is 1/8. Whatever the background beliefs are which cause together with the pinkness of the envelope the belief of the boss, these beliefs are not knowledge, as is clear from the way we presented the story.

But – one might object – didn't Dretske say that *whatever* is caused by r's being F' is caused by the information r's being F' carries? Thus, does it really matter whether or not the boss' belief was caused in connection with any background beliefs (and thus irrelevant whether or not they count as knowledge)?

There certainly is a sloppiness in the formulation of externalism that makes people think so. Externalism does not mean that it is independent of the receiver what informational content a signal has. In fact, the knowledge of the receiver about the source is part of the definition of what the informational content of a signal is. In Dretske's own words: 'What one learns or can learn, from a signal (event, condition, or state of affairs), and hence the information carried by that signal, depends in part on what one already knows about the alternative possibilities' (Dretske 1981, 43). To overlook this is to overemphasize externalism beyond reasonableness. If this as well as the recursive character of Definition 3|2–2 is recognized, cases (i)-(iii) are not necessarily a threat to Dretske's theory.

Further Reading

There is quite a number of critical studies of Dretske's account of knowlede, most of which argue that Dretske will need to introduce some notion of justification into the account. Examples for this are

- J. Christopher Maloney, 'Dretske on Knowledge and Information', *Analysis* 43 (1983), 25-28.

and

- William Edward Morris, 'Knowledge and the Regularity Theory of Information', *Synthese* 82 (1990), 375-398.

A defense of Dretske's theory against some of his critics (including a more detailed discussion of the purported counterexamples we discussed in this chapter) is provided by

- Anthony Doyle, 'Is Knowledge Information-Produced Belief? A Defense of Dretske Against some Critics', *The Southern Journal of Philosophy* XXIII (1985), 33-46.

3|3 Perception, Belief, and the Problem of Misrepresentation

Perception

A loud noise is coming from the sky. Manuel, my cat, and I all look up to see where it's coming from. All three of us see a Boeing 747 over our heads, ready to land on the nearby airport. Although we all see the Boeing 747, only Manuel knows from the information we got from seeing it, that it was a Boeing 747. My cat knows from seeing it that it was a white, noisy, annoying thing, I, however, form the belief that it was an Airbus. My belief seems to be a misrepresentation of what I saw. We have already discussed what Dretske's story behind all this is, but will have a closer look at it now. We will learn that the phenomenon of misrepresentation is not yet well understood in informational semantics.

Telling the little story above, I said that my cat and Manuel both saw the Boeing 747 over our heads. Perception is often understood as a form of cognitve activity that recognizes, classifies and distinguishes things. Certainly the cat did not classify the Boeing that it saw *as* a Boeing 747, only Manuel did. Dretske distinguishes two ways of decsribing our perceptions (Dretske 1969, 1989), one is extensional, the other intensional.

Extensionally speaking (or non-epistemically speaking), we take notice of the experiences we have when we see, hear or taste things. At this stage of our processing of sensory information, the internal state Manuel, the cat, and I are in is relevantly similar. It does code information, viz. information about the source of the noise coming from above, but it codes it in *analog* form. In this stage none of us knows yet *that* it is a Boeing 747, intensionally speaking.

In the extensional mode we describe what objects we are getting information about – this was more or less the same for Manuel, the cat, and me. The difference comes in when we describe what information (about the plane) each of us has succeeded in cognitively processing (that it was a Boeing 747).

> Our experience of the world is rich in information in a way that our consequent beliefs (if any) are not. A normal child of two can see as well as I can (probably better): The child's experience of the world is (I rashly conjecture) as rich and variegated as that of the most knowledgeable adult. What is lacking is a capacity to explot these experiences in the generation of reliable beliefs (knowledge) about what the child sees. I, my daughter, and my dog can all see the daisy. I see it as a daisy. My daughter sees it simply as a flower. And who knows about my dog? (Dretske 1983, 231)

Of course, what makes all the difference between Manuel, my cat, and me is not the sensory representation, which is, arguably, relevantly similar, but what we do with it. Cognitive processing of this information means throwing information away. Perception gives us the rich sensory representation, yet unstructured, in analog form. Now, when Manuel isolates one component of this information, that it is a Boeing 747, he *digitalizes* the analog information he has. He takes one piece of information away from the richer matrix of the sensory representation and features it to the exclusion of all these. We have to delete information in order to arrive at knowledge or recognition. Acquiring concepts is learning what information has to be thrown away and what has to be extracted from the sensory representations. "Until that happens, we can see but we do not believe" (Dretske 1983, 233).

Belief

As we have said already in the preceeding chapter, beliefs are structures with a content. Structures with content are something that we are also already familar with, namely information-bearing structures with an informational content. However, beliefs and information-bearing structures are quite different things.

First of all, the informational content of an information-bearing structure is too unspecific to qualify as the content of a belief. We have already seen that the information a structure carries includes everything which is nomically or analytically nested in whatever information it carries. Thus a structure that carries the information that there is water in the glass, also carries the information that there is H_2O in the glass, but the belief that there is water in the glass does not automatically have as its content that there is H_2O in the glass. I can believe that there is water in the glass without also believeing that there is H_2O in the glass, e.g. if I am ignorant of the fact that water is H_2O.

Secondly, informational content is factive. Nothing can have the informational content that s is F unless s is F. Unfortunately, beliefs are not like that. Beliefs can misrepresent things. This can be seen in the story considered above. I misclassified the object I saw as an Airbus, when in fact it was a Boeing 747.

Semantic Content

To solve the first problem, Dretske distinguishes between two ways of representing facts in the manner we have mentioned above already: analog and digital representation.

> **Definition 3|3–1**
>
> *S* carries the information that *t* is *F* in digital form iff
>
> > (i) *S* carries the information that *t* is *F*,
>
> and
>
> > (ii) there is no other piece of information, *t* is *K*, which is such that the information that *t* is *F* is nested in *t*'s being *K*, but not vice versa.

This gives us the most specific information that a structure carries about *t*.

As we have seen, carrying information is occupying an intentional state. Dretske's idea is to distinguish different orders of intentionality and different corresponding kinds of content and then to specify beliefs as these structures which have a high order of intentionality. The different orders of intentionality are defined as being closed to different degrees under nesting:

> **Definition 3|3–2**
>
> A signal S has informational content (content exhibiting the first order of intentionality) iff it is consistent to assume that it has the content that t is F, that all F's are G's and that S does not have the content that t is G.

> **Definition 3|3–3**
>
> A signal S has content exhibiting the second order of intentionality iff it is consistent to assume that it has the content that t is F, that it is a natural law that all F's are G's and that S does not have the content that t is G.

> **Definition 3|3–4**
>
> A signal S has semantic content (exhibiting the third order of intentionality) iff it is consistent to assume that it has the content that t is F, that it is analytically necessary that all F's are G's and that S does not have the content that t is G.

The semantic content of a signal t is then identified with the information t carries in digital form (Dretske 1981, 177.):

> **Definition 3|3–5**
>
> A structure S has the fact that t is F as its semantic content $=_{df}$
>
> > (a) S carries the information that t is F and
> >
> > (b) S carries no other piece of information, r is G, which is such that the information that t is F is nested (nomically or analyti-

> cally) in *r*'s being *F*.

But if semantic structures are so defined, there is clearly no room for error. If the semantic content that *s* is *F* requires *s* to be *F*, no belief can have semantic content unless it is true.

Misrepresentation

But, unfortunately, some of our beliefs are false, so belief can't be semantic structures. Although false beliefs have a determinate content (e.g. that there is a cow in front of me), they misrepresent how things stand (it's a horse, in fact). But how can we explain this in informational semantics? Informational semantics holds that – as we have seen – representation is a kind of causation or correlation, at least in case of perceptual beliefs. But how can a representation be caused by or be correlated with a state of affairs that does not obtain, i.e. can there be belief without knowledge?

In the preceeding chapter we hinted already at one way towards a solution. If we can make a type/token distinction, it seems possible to explain how a sign can have a certain determinate content and yet be false. What we have to assure is that it is representation types which are responsible for a sign's content independent of the environmental facts that determine the truth or falsity of the token sign. Because the representation is of such and such type it represents that a cow is in front of me, because of how things are in my surroundings it is false. Unfortunately things are not that easy.

The Disjunction Problem

Consider state type S. S is a state I can be in. What we aim to say is that S is correlated with the external state that c is B, which is shorthand for the external state that there is a cow in front of me. Now, for some reason (bad lighting conditions, forgot glasses, too much *Pilsener Urquell*, etc.) a token of S is caused by c's being D (say, a horse which is in front of me, a small brown one with a cow-like attitude towards grass and its surroundings). What we hope to say is that S is a misrepresentation now, because S *as a type* represents that c is B (that there is a cow).

But how can we say that? If the fact that c is D (the horse) can cause an S-token what reasons did we have in the first place to isolate tokens of the type c is B (cow) as privileged causal influences on my state S?

The most reliable correlation does not seem to obtain between c's being B and S nor between c's being D and S, but between S and (c is B ∨ c is D). But, and this is the problem, if the latter is the most reliable correlation, this should rather be the privileged one we should isolate as being the content of S! Now, S as a type represents that c is B or c is D. A token of S caused by c's being D is not an error anymore; we failed to explain how misrepresentations can occur.

It is difficult to solve this problem and some have argued that it is even unsolvable in principle for informational semantics. We will briefly review some of the possible options.

Situation One = Learning Period

One way philosophers have searched for a solution is to make a distinction between a learning period in which an organism is learning a concept and the period afterwards. This solution belongs to a class of solutions that try to distinguish two types of situations, viz. those situations (Situation One) in which the signal type gets its content (where the reliable correlation must be situated) and the situations (Situation Two) in which misrepresentation can occurr. The particular solution we are looking at now identifies the Situation One with the learning period.

During the learning period a representation type S acquires its content (by being caused by c's being B, say), but after the learning period is over, tokens of the type which are perhaps differently caused (by c's being D, say) do not contribute anymore to the content of the type. A token of type S which is then caused by c's being D is a misrepresentation, due to the correlation that obtained in the learning period between S and c's being B. This is Dretske's original approach, but it is doubtfull whether it really can solve the problem.

For the approach to work, Dretske has to enforce a strict distinction between what happens in and what happens after the learning period. The correlations that the learning period establishes determine what S represents, a teacher or reinforcement mechanism will have to ensure that the correlation so established is the right one, i.e. the tokens of S must be correlated with *c*s' being B. But not only do the actually obtaining correlations determine this, also the possibly obtaining correlations will matter (all cows shall fall under 'cow' not only the ones met during the learning period).

As Jerry Fodor has argued it is first of all unclear whether the strict distinction between learning period and the time after is principled in any way, it seems certainly not as principled as the distinction between truth and falsity. But, and that is more damaging to Dretske's account, the fix doesn't even seem to work. Consider my acquisition of R tokens in S circumstances during the training period. The concept I try to acquire is COW and during the learning period all works very well, 'cow'-tokenings are all and only elicited by cows. Now the learning period comes to an official end (I receive a document saying 'Daniel has successfully acquired the concept COW. Congratulations! Yours, the reinforcement mechanism.').

Now I am free to run around and misapply the concept. The first thing I meet after heavy celebration of my fresh acquired concept (presumably being a bit tipsy from too much *Pilsener Urquell*), is a horse (a token of T, we will say) which is in front of me, a small brown one with a cow-like attitude towards grass and its surroundings. I produce a 'cow'-token in causal consequence. If all would work well, this horse-elicited 'cow'-token should now be wild and have the false content that there is a cow in front of me. But it is not clear how it could have this, Dretske's solution seems to ignore relevant counterfactuals.

What if a T-token had occurred during the training period? Well, presumably it would have elicited a tokening of R, just as it did that evening after the period was over. But then, of course, this is a counterfactual relevant for the learning period. If T is a situation that, if it had occurred during training, would have been sufficient for R, the correlation established is not one between R and S, but really between R and the disjunction (T ∨ S).

But then we have the old disjunction problem again. If the training really established a correlation between (T ∨ S), the content of R really *is* (T ∨ S). So the tokening of 'cow' caused by the little horse is no wild tokening after all, and therefore it is not false. A token with the content (COW ∨ SMALL HORSE) is true when there is a small horse.

A possible reply for Dretske could be to accuse Fodor of having overlooked relevant counterfactuals himself, viz. that my teacher would have disapproved of T-elicited R-responses if they had occurred during the learning period. But such a reply might undermine the whole enterprise to explain the content of a symbol or a structure in terms of correlations between these structures and the world, rather than between structures and the intentions of teachers. We will not pursue the matter here, but turn to an alternative way to solution from the same class of solutions.

Situation One = Normal Conditions

The basic intuition behind this class of solutions is that if misrepresentation occurs, something must have gone wrong. In normal situations 'cow' would be triggered by cows, not by small horses. It is the abnormality of the situation (it is dark, etc.) that is responsible for my mistake. If we can tell the normal situations apart from the abnormal ones, we could get the correlation problem fixed. If the correlation occurrs in normal situations, then the correlation establishes semantic content, if not, then the tokenings elicited in the situation are free to be false. OK, but what is a normal situation? Doesn't this talk bring back the intentionality that naturalism tries to avoid?

> The basic form of teleological versions of informational semantics is as follows: some causal chains resulting in tokens of a representation type are normal, and some are wild. Only normal causal chains contribute to the content of the representation type. What makes a causal chain wild is either the breakdown of the proper functioning of the organism's perceptual and psychological mechanisms, or else some environmental abnormality. A cow does not cause you to think 'horse' without something going wrong some-

where, and when something goes wrong somewhere, that causal chain is irrelevant to the representation type's content. (Godfrey-Smith 1989, 541.)

Of course, the talk of 'proper functions' and 'teleology' is assumed to be naturalized by reference to evolutionary theory. The proper function of a mechanism of some organism is what the mechanism was selected for (the mechanism's contribution to the (still) being there of the organism). It should be noted, however, that the proper functions in question are functions of the belief forming mechanisms rather than the beliefs themselves, who do not seem to have proper functions. Anyway, the idea is this (following the exposition given by Fodor 1990, 70):

If a frog sticks out his tongue at a fly, there is a state S of the frog's nervous system such that

(i) S is reliably caused by flies in normal circumstances;

(ii) S is the normal cause of an ecologically appropriate, fly-directed response;

(iii) evolution bestowed S on frogs because (i) and (ii) are true of it.

The state S normally resonates to flies, and it is because of that, that the frog has this device, viz. a mechanism that brings about S states (it is the proper function of the mechanism producing S). Finally, that S means FLY in normal as well as in abnormal circumstances (in which it is not flies but something else to which the S-tokens are resonating) is only because of all that.

There are some doubts, however, that this proposal is going to help out. One reason is that Mother Nature doesn't really care whether the frog has FLY or (FLY ∨ FAKE FLY PUT INTO MY VISUAL FIELD BY ANNOYING BIOLOGIST) represented as long as, normally, enough flies are eaten. Moreover, Mother Nature does not discriminate between reliably equivalent contents. 'Darwin cares how many flies you eat but not what description you eat them under.' (Fodor 1990, 73.). If so, it might be doubted that evolutionary teleology can reconstruct the intentionality of mentals states (intensional contexts, in particular).

Another problem is the problem of frequent false alarm. Frequent false alarm can be a good thing for a beast. Rats – for example – tend to generalize hastily when it comes to poisonous food, scorpions strike for mechanical waves in the sand for prey. In all these cases it is normal that the sign is poorly correlated with its truth condition (normally there is no prey in the sand, normally donuts are not poisonous for rats although the one yesterday was followed by a bad stomach right after, etc.):

> [Teleological approaches] would be troubled if there were cases where we aim to take a representation to indicate a certain environmental state, when it is not just unlikely now that the state obtains, given the presence of the sign, but when it is ecologically normal that the state is unlikely to obtain, given the presence of the sign. There is trouble if it can be normal that a sign is poorly correlated with its truth condition. (Godfrey-Smith 1989, 547.)

We will not go into this. Nevertheless, we shall briefly look at one more option before we close the chapter.

Asymmetric Dependence
Jerry Fodor has developed a treatement of error in informational semantics which involves no appeal to teleology. As the teleosemantic account and Dretske's own approach, Fodor regards some possible tokens of a representation type as wild or abnormal. Such tokens are not contributing to the content of the type and therefore are misrepresentations. Now, it seems that the little horse caused the 'cow'-tokening in me, because 'cow'-tokenings are caused by cows and the little horse looked pretty much like a cow at that moment. If there had not been any cows ever, there had been no 'cow'-token the horse could have caused. That horses can cause me to say 'cow' depends on the fact that cows cause me to say 'cow', but not on the fact that horses do. This seems to be an asymmetrical dependence between the normal and the abnormal causes of the tokenings. What makes the dependence asymmetrical is, of course, causality. The 'cow'-state was shaped by

cows, not by little horse, and therefore means COW. We will not discuss Fodor's theory here (you can find a discussion in the paper by Godfrey-Smith in the Further Reading-section). But what is emphasized by Fodor, and maybe of some interest for the very last chapter of the book, is that although a lot of information is around in the world, there does not have to be that much meaning around as well. Information needs causal covariance, meaning seems to involve something more, namely asymmetric dependence.

Further Reading

This chapter is again based on Dretske's *Knowledge and the Flow of Information*. For the problem of misrepresentation in informational semantics we refer the interested reader to

- Peter Godfrey-Smith, 'Misinformation', in: *Canadian Journal of Philosophy* 19 (1989), 533-550.

- Jerry Fodor, *A Theory of Content and Other Essays*, Cambridge./Mass. (MIT Press) 1992.

For teleosemantics ('proper function', 'normal situation') in particular, we suggest

- Ruth Millikan, Language, *Thought, and Other Biological Categories. New Foundations for Realism*, Cambridge/Mass. (MIT Press) 1984.

- David Papineau, *Philosophical Naturalism*, Oxford (Blackwell) 1993.

4 | Situation Theory and Information
Bringing Ontology back into Information Theory

ONE of the main ideas in the last chapter was that information is out there in the world. Being investigative does not mean creating facts, but exploring what the world (reality) is like. Information is not generated then, but found. The circumstances investigated already contain the information that is to be brought to light, or, in as much as it is just there in the clear sun light, is to be broadcasted to some audience.

If information is out there in the world (reality) this cannot mean that some symbols or sentences are lying around in the sun. We use symbols and sentences to extract information. We use symbols and sentences to express information. Information, however, precedes the formulation of sentences.

What then does it mean that information *is* there somewhere? Are there some strange (ethereal) pellets to be collected by the information scientists? Are these the *pieces* of information you were told to collect? As a hard nosed, tough minded reader of logic books you certainly do not believe in that story. Now, where then in particular is the information? You might say that it is where the objects are that the piece of information is about. Nice try, but this brings us directly to – ontology.

Ontology (or if you like to call it *metaphysics*) had a bad press in the days of Logical Positivism (where the semantic approach originated). Metaphysical question were considered not to be real questions, but related to a *choice* of language. Given some language and its logical framework (especially its quantificational variables) ontological matters of the broadest category were considered to be dealt with conclusively. Within some language the 'only' questions that remained were which *kinds* of objects you allow to quantify over, these you introduce into your theory's ontology (a usage of 'ontology' in a narrow sense related to competing theories like corpuscle physics or phlogiston theory). Philosophy – unfortunately – has its fashions as well, and ontology is on the rise again.

We have already seen in Chapter 2|3 that working within a fine grained ontological framework might have something to it. We might be able to solve the problem of the informational content of logical truths.

Situation semantics was introduced in the early 1980s to 'bring ontology back to semantics'. This was considered to be a fruitful research program supposedly more apt to treat or even solve long standing problems in the philosophy of language and the semantics of propositional attitudes (like ascriptions of beliefs and desires).

Here we will consider bringing ontology back to information theory. This will be an ontology of the units of information, so called *infons*. To set out the theory of infons and their fine grained logical structure one needs an ontology of the world (reality) that corresponds to the structures we find in infons. That is the link to old fashioned ontology, concerned with the ultimate or penultimate building blocks of reality. These building blocks may not only include the objects and properties we have in First Order Logic, but also locations, times, polarities and more eccentric types of entities to be introduced by some abstraction principles.

The ontology outlined here, therefore, comes as a package consisting on the one hand of a theory of situations (as real pieces of the world) and on the other hand of a theory of infons (as real pieces of information).

4 | 1   The Framework of Situation Semantics

Situation semantics was introduced in the early 80s by Jon Barwise and John Perry. It was originally motivated (Barwise 1981) as a realistic approach to a semantics of naked infinitive perceptual reports like

(1)   Austin saw a man get shaved in Oxford.

The semantics of such perceptual reports pose a problem for the classical approach. The classical, Fregean, doctrine is that the referent of a sentence (and also of an embedded naked infinitive) is a truth value. But the embedded infinitives do not seem to refer to truth values but rather to situations or scenes (perceptually registered situations). In contrast to an embedded that-clause, like

(2)   Austin saw that a man got shaved in Oxford.

(1) does not demand from Austin any command of concepts or other knowledge (Austin could be the man's dog, for example, waiting in front of the barber shop). (1) is veridical and extensional whereas (2) is not. Moreover, naked infinitives behave differently than the corresponding that-clauses with respect to negation. All this convinced Barwise and Perry that there must be something wrong with the Fregean picture.

Keith Devlin developed situation semantics into a theory of information (units). Since we are concerned with information here we follow Devlin's way of exposition. Later on situation semantics was developed into a formal model of information flow by Jon Barwise and Jerry Seligman. Chapter 5 will deal with their models.

What does 'Bringing Ontology Back into Information Theory' mean? The theories considered so far were syntactic, semantic or were concerned with epistemic properties of information. Situation semantics' slogan was 'bringing ontology back to semantics': definitions and explanations are based on a plethora of ontological categories. This applies to an analysis of information in terms of situation semantics as well.

Basic Ontology
The basic ontology includes:

Basic Ontology
individuals, denoted by a, b, c...
relations, denoted by P, Q, R...
spatial locations, denoted by l, l', l"...
temporal locations, denoted by t, t', t"
situations, denoted by s, s', s"...
truth values: 1 (true) and 0 (false) [also called polarities]
Space (time) regions have basic relations:
l ° l'   i.e. l overlaps l'   (in space)
l ~ l'   i.e. l precedes l'   (respectively t ~ t')
t @ t'   i.e. t overlaps t'   (in time)

Situations are of course central to situation semantics – but what is a situation? Are situations abstract or concrete entities?

The most important feature of situations is: they are partial (not total, as possible worlds are). Situations tell us about some objects and some properties we could talk about, say that Fido is a dog. A situation – in distinction to a possible world – need not tell us about all predicates whether or not they apply to Fido (whether Fido is brown, sleeping, running etc.). If some situation does not tell us that Clara is a cat, we cannot conclude that the world is such that Clara is not a cat, all we know that it is not part of that situation we are looking at at the moment that Clara is a cat. This limitation of our model to a partial representation of knowledge is one of the main virtues of situation semantics.

Situation semanticists speak of 'situations', 'abstract situations', 'situation types', 'facts', 'propositions' and 'infons'. Sometimes they have changed their terminology! So what should 'situation' refer to? Situations are parts of reality (the universe). Here we take (following Devlin in some of his remarks) situations as *concrete* entities. An example for a situation is:

> Peter Kaputnik's clock is white in Trento, 8/5/2002 at 8 a.m.

If you take a part of the universe you have a situation s (involving some individuals, relations, and a location), s being partial. So what really is telling us something about a part of the world is not the situation itself – as we loosely said two paragraphs before – but a *description* of that situation. The situation is part of the world, the description of the situation is part of the world description. 'Abstract situation' etc. are constructed to classify situations (as concrete entities) with respect to their possible descriptions. For the moment think of an abstract situation as, for example, someone's clock being white in Trento. There will be several situations that fall in that category determined by the abstract situation (one taking place on 8/5/2002 at 8 a.m. involving Peter Kaputnik, another one, say, on 9/8/2002 at 7.45 p.m. involving Luciano Parti).

Types and Parameters

To introduce more complex entities we need some more basic categories:

> **Types and Parameters**
>
> For each object of the theory there is at least one type which it is an object of. Basic types are:
> - TIM: the type of temporal locations (respectively LOC)
> - IND: the type of an individual
> - SIT: the type of a situation
> - REL^n: the type of an n-place relation
>
> For each basic type there is an infinite collection of basic parame-

> ters.
>> a^* is a parameter for individuals
>> s^* is a parameter for situations
>> t^* is a parameter for a time region, etc.
>
> We write 'x:T' to say that x is of type T.

We explain infons in a minute, but to show what parameters are good for, just think of infons as containing some information about some situation. We say that a situation *supports* some infon, if the situation is as the infon says. We write '$s \models \phi$' for this. (It is, of course, an analogy to the relation of a sentence being made true by a model/world.)

Now, given parameters we can introduce more types by *type abstraction*:

$$[x^* \mid s \models I]$$

This type is the type of those x for which situation s supports the infons in the set of infons I (in which infons contain a parameter x^*). For example:

$$[x^* \mid s_1 \models \langle\langle dog, x^*, \text{Trento}, 8/5/2002\ 7\ \text{a.m.}, 1 \rangle\rangle]$$

This is the type of objects which are dogs in Trento on May, 8th, 2002 at 7 in the morning, given some situation s_1 (supposedly in Trento). (We explain the notation after the '$\models$' in a minute.)

Parameters work like variables: they can be anchored to objects of their type. An *anchor* for a set A of basic parameters is a function f defined on A which assigns to each parameter T_n in A an object of Type T.

Taking our primitive categories we introduce *infons* (by giving a schematic example):

$$\langle\langle R, a_1, ..., a_n, l_i, t_j, 1\rangle\rangle$$

A simple infon says that some objects stand in some relation or that they do not. It contains places for the relation or property in question, for the objects which stand in that relation or which have that property, for the time and the location, and a *polarity* (i.e. a truth value indicating whether the instantiation of the property or relation does take place or not). So in the scheme given, the place of the '1' could be taken by a '0'.

Given some infon we can introduce the *abstract situation* defining the type of situations that support that infon, for example:

$$[s^* \mid s^* \vDash \phi]$$

We abstract here on the situation parameter within a support relation. A situation is of that type if it supports the infon φ (i.e. is such that φ obtains).

If φ' contains parameters (i.e. is a parametric, not a complete infon) then the type T = $[s^* \mid s^* \vDash \phi']$ is a parametric type and φ' the *conditioning infon* of that type T [*cond*(T) = φ']. φ' has to be anchored to yield a factor complete infon. If f is an anchor defined on all parameters of φ', we can have $s \vDash \phi'[f]$, the situation s supports φ' as anchored by this specific anchor f.

Given infons we can also introduce *propositions*:

$$s \vDash \phi$$

A proposition says that some infon is factual. An infon φ 'is made factual' by a situation s if s is a real situation which is as infon φ says it is. s supports φ. So information is always about a situation.

We can say that infon σ is *a fact* iff the world is as σ says: For a *real s*, $s \vDash \sigma$.

So we have situations, situation types (giving abstract situations by abstracting on the situation parameter), propositions, infons, facts – and they are all different from each other.

An infon cannot only have objects as its arguments. It can also contain parameters. This gives us a *parametric infon* like

$\langle\langle dog, x^*, \text{Trento}, 8/5/2002\ 7\ \text{a.m.}, 1\rangle\rangle$

We can now say what an anchor does: If γ is a infon and f an anchor for some parameter in γ, $\gamma[f]$ denotes the infon resulting from replacing each parameter a^* in $\text{dom}(f)$ by $f(a^*)$. (Compare interpreting variables in a formula.) For example $\langle\langle dog, \text{Fido}, \text{Trento}, 8/5/2002\ 7\ \text{a.m.}, 1\rangle\rangle$ is the anchoring of the parametric infon achieved by anchoring 'x^*' to Fido (i.e. $f(x^*) = \text{Fido}$). Given a condition φ, $a^*|\varphi$ is a restricted parameter, open only to be anchored to objects that fulfil the condition φ. (A condition being a conjunction of infons.)

We can go one step further. We said situations are concrete entities, so situations can be contained in infons, e.g.

$\langle\langle see, \text{David}, s', l', t', 1\rangle\rangle$

According to this (schematic) infon David sees situation s' (say a football match) at time t' in location l'.

(Since situations support infons this embedding of situations in infons might lead to semantic paradoxes, but we will not care about this here.)

Infon Logic

Compound infons are defined by closing infons under conjunction, disjunction, and bounded quantification (over parameters):

$\varphi \wedge \sigma$, for example, is a compound infon. We can state semantic rules for evaluating compound infons with respect to some situation (i.e. give supporting conditions in analogy to truth conditions for complex sentences).

For any s: $s \models \varphi \wedge \sigma$ iff $s \models \varphi$ and $s \models \sigma$.

For any s: $s \models \varphi \vee \sigma$ iff $s \models \varphi$ or $s \models \sigma$

Note: Infons are not closed under negation! So we have no rule like

(*)   For any s: $s \not\models \langle\langle P, a, 1 \rangle\rangle \rightarrow s \models \langle\langle P, a, 0 \rangle\rangle$

Situations supporting infons (giving propositions) are not negation complete. Situation semantics argues that it is sufficient and fruitful to start with partial descriptions or partial information. Therefore the polarities in the infons have to do the work of negation, but $s \models \langle\langle cat, c, 1 \rangle\rangle$ does not imply $s \models \langle\langle cat, c, 0 \rangle\rangle$.

If φ is an infon that contains the parameter x^* and A is some set of objects, then

$$(\exists x^* \in A) \, \varphi$$

is a compound infon. So for a situation s that contains the members of A:

$s \models (\exists x^* \in A) \, \varphi$ iff there is an anchor f of x^* to an element of A, such that $s \models \varphi[f]$.

Accordingly for $(\forall x^* \in A)$.

Infons were introduced into situation semantics by Keith Devlin. They correspond to what Barwise and Perry – most of the time – call 'situations'. Note that infons are something like ordered tuples, which means that an infon really contains *the entities* which make it up. We are not talking about linguistic, but about ontological constructions. The 'dog' in the example above is not the predicate of some language, but the property of being a dog; 'Fido' is not the name, but the dog himself. Infons are no linguistic entities. Only the limits of putting some representation on a page makes them look like sentences of a formal language. Sometimes some expressions are *mentioned* in an infon, but only just like objects are parts of infons (mentioned expressions are objects, namely the signs usually *used* to say something). The theory of information presented is therefore independent of language and a specific coding scheme! This is just the opposite in the syntactic and possible worlds approach; they are both relative to some L_i. We like infons, since we are after information and information flow.

Fine Grained Information

The ontological approach of situation semantics allows for more fine grained informational content than in other approaches.

The syntactic approach only very indirectly (by the definition of the coding scheme) talks about semantic content at all. The possible worlds approach gives the same informational content to all contingent statements (in case of an a priori measure)!

Given an approach that bases information on the structure of information bearing entities you can make finer distinctions. The infon i_1

(i_1) $\langle\langle happy, \text{Peter}, t', l', 1\rangle\rangle$

has another informational content than i_2

(i_2) $\langle\langle happy, \text{Helga}, t', l', 1\rangle\rangle$

because i_1 involves Peter and i_2 involves Helga.

Abstract situations

Let us once again look at abstract situations. They could also be introduced as sets of infons like:

$\{\sigma \mid s \vDash \sigma\}$

An abstract situation is then defined as the set of infons that are made real by a situation of that kind. Not all abstract situations are instantiated (e.g., some might be inconsistent due to the combination of infons they include).

Situation types like:

$$[s^* \mid s^* \vDash \sigma]$$

have the same purpose. For example:

$$[s^* \mid s^* \vDash \langle\langle running, a^*, l', t', 1 \rangle\rangle]$$

is the type of situation where some individual is running in l' at t'.

The relation of support can be applied to abstract situations: Let s be an *abstract* situation, now we have:

$$s \vDash \sigma \text{ iff } \sigma \in s.$$

(which might remind you of a basic fact, *Lindenbaum's Lemma*, about linguistic possible worlds).

Abstract situations, however, have other functions as well. Relative to abstract situations we can now explain what it means that one real situation *is part* of another real situation: Let s_{1a}, s_{2a} be the abstract situations that contain all infons supported by the situations s_1 and s_2,

$$s_1 \text{ is part of } s_2 \text{ iff } s_{1a} \subseteq s_{2a}.$$

If some real situation is part of another real situation, then the larger one (the one it is a part of) contains all the entities and relations of the first situation. So the larger one supports at least as many infons as does the situation which is a part of it. So the set of infons supported by the situation being the part has to be a subset of the set of infons supported by the larger situation. (The support relation is monotonic: extending a situation to a larger situation does not cancel the support for some infon. Monotonicity would not hold in this case if situations were negation complete.)

A *course of events* is a partial function from the product of space and time regions into situation types with space and time parameters. It tells a partial history of the universe. (A minimal one changes one situation into another.) Like situations, courses of events are not total (they are not negation complete world histories like in some modal logics).

Getting Information

To model information flow we need a cognitive system. A cognitive system is an object that is capable of having knowledge:

 The system is able to extract digital information from analogue representations of its environment (cf. Chapter 3|3 on Dretske).

 The system then can use its initial information to derive more information by some mechanisms (here called *constraints*).

Constraints link situations. Constraints are used in situation semantics to model (natural) laws, conventions, and other kinds of regularities.
Constraints are relations between types of situations. For example:

Smoke means fire.

That is: If S_1 is the type of situations where smoke is present, and S_2 is the type of situations where there is fire, these situations are linked by a (natural) constraint. An agent can pick up information (that there is a situation of type S_2) by observing that there is a situation of type S_1 if the agent is aware of or attuned to the constraint.
Constraints can be written:

$$S' \Rightarrow S''$$

where S' and S'' are situation types.
Constraints are involved in meaning relations as well; for example: 'fire' means fire. This is a constraint linking an utterance situation type to a type of situation where fire is present. Attuned agents with respect

THE FRAMEWORK OF SITUATION SEMANTICS

to this constraint understand the expression 'fire'. The situation semantics account of meaning, therefore, is based on constraints. The constraints give information what other kind of situation is involved here.

Let us look at the example in more detail: The situation types mentioned can be modelled:

$$S = [s^* | s^* \models \langle\langle smokey, t^*, 1 \rangle\rangle]$$

$$S' = [s^* | s^* \models \langle\langle fiery, t^*, 1 \rangle\rangle]$$

$$S'' = [s^{*'} | s^{*'} \models (\langle\langle speaking, a^*, t^*, 1\rangle\rangle \wedge \langle\langle utters, a^*, \text{'fire'}, t^*, 1\rangle\rangle)]$$

with the two constraints

(C1) $S \Rightarrow S'$

and

(C2) $S'' \Rightarrow S'$

Any instance where a constraint is *utilised* making an inference about an object x^* involves specific situations by anchoring.

We are not concerned with the analysis of meaning here, but to give an example of using the notion of constraint to explain sentential meaning: Let σ be the sentence 'I am eating now.' The meaning of σ (||σ||) is the constraint linking the following situation types:

$$[s'^* | s'^* \models \{\langle\langle speak, a^*, t^*, 1\rangle\rangle, \langle\langle say, a^*, \sigma, t^*, 1\rangle\rangle\}]$$

$$[s''^* | s''^* \models \langle\langle eat, a^*, t^*, 1\rangle\rangle]$$

In the first type (in distinction to S'' above note the curly brackets) we have a *set* of infons supported by a situation. In one of these infons (like in S'') an expression as mentioned is present as an argument. The constraint linking these two situation types tells us: If individual a utters σ at time t that individual is eating at that time.

Information Flow (the Idea)

We look closer at information flow in the next chapter, but having available the concept of constraint we can understand the idea of information flow within situation semantics. Consider the constraints and situation types we just have given, say

(C1) $S \Rightarrow S'$

$S = [s^*|\ s^* \models \langle\langle smokey, t^*, 1\rangle\rangle]$,

$S' = [s^*|\ s^* \models \langle\langle fiery, t^*, 1\rangle\rangle]$

Suppose $s_1:S$ (i.e., situation s_1 is of type S). Being aware of the constraint (C1) we have the information that there is a situation s_2 (maybe $s_2 = s_1$) with $s_2:S'$ such that s_1 and s_2 are co-temporal, i.e. t^* has to be anchored to the same time interval. We get information about some situation given that we know that a given situation is of some type and that type is linked by a constraint to some other type (of situation). The actual linking of situations is done by parameters (where a parameter which is present in the two situation types is anchored to an object present in the two situations linked).

To see that some infons are supported by some situation s' given what we know about some other situation s and being aware of or being attuned to constraints C, C'... is to acquire knowledge (in an externalist epistemology). You can acquire knowledge without being aware of it or the acquiring process. Knowledge is independent of its mode of representation (see chapter 3|2).

Information

Then what, according to situation semantics, is information after all?

 The information an agent *a* has about a situation *s* is the closure of *a*'s representations of *s* under infon logic given the constraints that *a* is aware of or attuned to.

 The information present in a situation *s* is the closure of the set of infons supported by *s* under infon logic given all constraints.

Information is present in the world. So we should expect a theory that speaks mainly about the (ontological) structures of the world.

Situation semantics is mainly an ontologically new theory: linguistic phenomena are treated equally well in other approaches closer to traditional possible worlds semantics, e.g. in Categorical Grammar ('Montague-Grammar', cf. Montague 1974, Cann 1993). Critics have claimed situation semantics should not be considered psychologically real; with respect to human cognitive mechanisms it is said to be naïve and uninformed (cf. Jackendoff 1985, 1997). Taking situations seriously we considered them as concrete entities. But not all infons are actual. If you consider a situation type $[s \mid s \vDash \sigma]$ where σ is not realized in the actual world/the universe, what does the '*s*' refer to? It cannot refer to actual situations, since the infon is not factual. So it seems to refer to possible, but not actual situations that support an infon that is not factual, but could be. Since we take situations to be concrete entities this commits us to possible concrete entities: *possibilia* in the full sense of it. Situation semantics becomes a version of genuine modal realism in the fashion of Lewis (Lewis 1986)! If one does not restrict the forming of abstract situations the ontological plenty of situation semantics is not only one of categories (situations, individuals, properties...) but one of modalities.

Nevertheless: Situation semantics might model one aspect of situational information flow. Information flow can be represented at such an abstract level of logical (or conceptual) analysis. That is where we are.

Further Reading

A readable introduction with an eye to the concept of information is:

 📖 Keith Devlin, *Logic and Information*, Cambridge/Mass. 1991.

The classic is:

 📖 Jon Barwise/John Perry, *Situations and Attitudes*, Cambridge/Mass. 1983.

although it contains some different terminology and notation. For a discussion of Barwise's and Perry's early work, see volume 8 of *Linguistics and Philosophy* (1985), 1-161, which is dedicated to *Situations and Attitudes*. See also

 📖 Sten Lindström, 'Critical study of Jon Barwise and John Perry, *Situations and Attitudes*' *Noûs* XXV, 743-770.

You can find the broader context and some applications of situation semantics in a collection of papers by Jon Barwise:

 📖 Jon Barwise, *The Situation in Logic*. Stanford 1988.

and the two volumes of:

 📖 Robin Cooper/Kuniaki Mukai/John Perry (eds.), *Situation Theory and Its Applications*, 2 Volumes, Stanford 1990.

(There you can find, for example, an account of Infon Logic by Jon Barwise and John Etchemendy, 'Information, Infons, and Inference'.)

4|2 Information Architecture and Constraints

Introduction

Based on the ideas contained in situation theory, John Perry and David Israel further developed an account of information and informational content. Since the principles they discuss are also the background of the more technical developments discussed in the rest of this book we will repeat them here and briefly explicate the ideas behind them. We hope this will help to tie together what you have learned until now about situation semantics and externalism with the information flow framework of the next chapter.

Intuitive Principles of Information

We will explain information flow in terms of situation semantics with the help of some rather simple examples taken from Perry and Israel's papers on the matter. We will begin with some terminology. Have a look at the following sentences:

(1)   The x-ray indicates that Jackie has a broken leg.

(2)   The fact that the x-ray has such and such a pattern indicates that Jackie has a broken leg.

These are two examples of what we will call *information reports*. The information verb (here 'indicates', other examples are 'shows' or 'carries the information') and the preceding noun phrase are *information contexts*. The propositions referred to by the that-clauses are the *informational contents* reported, the object designated by the noun phrase in (1) is the *carrier of information*, the object designated by the noun phrase in (2) the *indicating fact*. Information reports in this sense are factive, i.e. when something indicates or shows or carries the information that A, then A. If an information report is true, then the informational content is true too.

Looking closer at the examples, we can notice that both are about Jackie and an x-ray. The x-ray is the carrier of information and it is a carrier because of a certain indicating fact, the fact that it has such and such a pattern. Thus it is facts that carry information. Facts are taken as some kind of infon. Let us generalize both observations:

(A) Facts carry information.

(B) The informational content of a fact is a true proposition.

In the last chapter we explained already what *constraints* in situation semantics are. Constraints are contingent matters of fact, that one situation involves another. If situations with smoke involve situations with fire, then smoke carries the information that there is fire. Facts thus carry information relative to constraints:

(C) The information a fact carries is relative to a constraint.

If the constraints are contingent matters of fact and could be different than they actually are, then the information a fact carries also could be different, given these other constraints:

(D) The information a fact carries is not an intrinsic property of it.

If we consider our examples again, we can also add that facts might carry information about remote things and remote situations. Archaeologists study facts of our days to get information about situations some thousand years ago. Facts about cosmic microwave background radiation that hits the earth tomorrow might carry information about situations in very remote areas of our universe a rather very long time ago:

(E) The informational content of a fact can concern remote things and situations.

INFORMATION ARCHITECTURE AND CONSTRAINTS 165

It is rather obvious that the constraints alone can't be the whole story. The x-ray carries the information that Jackie has a broken leg. This is because the x-ray has such and such a pattern and there is a constraint that dogs have broken legs whose x-rays have such and such a pattern. But that constraint is too general to carry information about Jackie. That the x-ray carries the information it does is not only due to its having a certain pattern, but also due to being taken of Jackie. This fact connects the *pure information* that the dog this x-ray is of had a broken leg when the x-ray was taken of Jackie. This is what we will call the *connecting fact*. These facts come into play when facts carry information about objects which are not part of the indicating fact. Such information is what we will call *incremental information*, this is the information carried by a signal relative to connecting facts.

(F) Informational content can be specific; the propositions that are informational contents can be about objects that are not part of the indicating fact.

(G) Indicating facts contain such information only relative to connecting facts; the information is incremental, given those facts.

What we are after is a theory of information flow. Information flow typically involves a variety of carriers, sound waves, electrical signals, lights, and vibrations that manage to bring a piece of information from the source to a receiver. That all these carriers can do so is because they are part of a communication channel that is constituted by a set of constraints, binding them all together.

(H) Many different facts, involving variations in objects, properties, relations and spatiotemporal locations, can indicate one and the same informational content – relative to the same or different constraints.

(I) Information can be stored and transmitted in a variety of forms.

Thus far we have considered information as an extrinsic fact about an agent, a device or a signal. Given different facts and constraints the information an agent has or a signal carries might be different from the way it actually is. But there is one thing that does not depend on remote contingencies, that is the good information does for the creatures using it:

(J) Having information is good; creatures whose behavior is guided or controlled by information (by their information carrying states) are more likely to succeed than those which are not so guided.

Information in Situation Semantics

Now we can construct a theory of information within the framework of situation semantics. We have said that the x-ray having such and such pattern carries pure information relative to a constraint and incremental information relative to a connecting fact. Let us first explicate *pure information* in situation theoretic terms:

> **Definition 4|2–1**
>
> Let C be some constraint, cond(T) a conditioning infon of T. The fact σ carries the pure information that P relative to C iff
>
> 1. $C = \langle\langle \text{Involves}, T, T', 1 \rangle\rangle$.
>
> 2. For any anchor f such that σ = $cond(T)[f]$, P = the proposition that $\exists s'\ (s' \models \exists a_{1},...a_{n}(cond(T')[f]))$.

The first clause states that for every situation of Type T there is one of type T'. Together with the second it states for our example that the x-ray's having such and such a pattern indicates that there is a dog of which this is an x-ray, and that dog has a broken leg.

From the pure information we want to get to the incremental information now. What we need is a notion of relative involvement, such that if T involves T' relative to T", then, for any pair of situations of the first and third types, there is a situation of the second type. Relative involvement is a ternary relation, the third type being the connecting type, the type of the connecting situation that we need to bring the pure information together with Jackie.

> Definition 4|2-2
>
> Let C be some relative constraint, *cond*(T) and *cond*(T") conditioning infons of T and T', respectively, then the fact σ *carries the incremental information that P relative to C and the fact* σ' iff
>
> 1. $C = \langle\langle \text{Involves}_R, T, T', T'', 1 \rangle\rangle$.
>
> 2. For any anchor f such that σ = *cond*(T)[f], ∧ σ' = cond(T")[f], P = the proposition that $\exists s'\ (s' \models \exists a_1,...a_n(cond(T')[f]))$.

In our example the connecting fact was that the x-ray is of Jackie. It is in virtue of this fact that Jackie, as the constituent of this fact is also a constituent of the proposition indicated, namely the proposition that it is Jackie's leg that is broken.

Details

To see in some detail how this theory deals with the case of Jackie, the x-ray and the broken leg, we will apply everything now formally. (As the above, the following follows closely Perry and Israel 1990.)

Let's first consider the x-ray case as a case of pure information. Then we have the following constraint: whenever there is a state of affairs consisting of some x-ray's having such and such a pattern at some time t, then there is a state of affairs involving a dog's leg having been the object of that x-ray and that leg's being broken at t.

So the indicated proposition is that there is a dog of which this is the x-ray, and it has a broken leg. The pure information is about the x-ray, but not about Jackie, or her leg.

$$T = [s \mid s \models \langle\langle \text{X-ray}, \mathbf{x}, \mathbf{t}; 1 \rangle\rangle \wedge \langle\langle \text{Has-pattern-}\Phi, \mathbf{x}, \mathbf{t}; 1 \rangle\rangle]$$

$$T' = [s \mid s \models \langle\langle \text{Is-xray-of}, \mathbf{x}, \mathbf{y}, \mathbf{t}; 1 \rangle\rangle \wedge \langle\langle \text{Has-broken-leg}, \mathbf{y}, \mathbf{t}; 1 \rangle\rangle]$$

$$C = \langle\langle \text{Involves}, T, T'; 1 \rangle\rangle$$

This gives us the constraint. Now we need the indicating situation, to satisfy T. The indicating situation, σ, is

$$\langle\langle \text{X-ray}, a, t'; 1 \rangle\rangle \wedge \langle\langle \text{Has-pattern-}\Phi, a, t'; 1 \rangle\rangle$$

where a is the x-ray and t' the time. We assume that σ is factual, that is that ∃s(s ⊨ σ). Let f be any anchor defined on **x** and **t** (at least) such that

$$\sigma = cond(T)[f] = \langle\langle \text{X-ray}, \mathbf{x}, \mathbf{t}, 1 \rangle\rangle \wedge \langle\langle \text{Has-pattern-}\Phi, \mathbf{x}, \mathbf{t}; 1 \rangle\rangle[f]$$

(Thus, $f(\mathbf{x}) = a$ and $f(\mathbf{t}) = t'$.) Then P = the proposition that ∃s'(s' ⊨ ∃y ($\langle\langle$ Is-xray-of, **x**, **y**, **t**; 1 $\rangle\rangle \wedge \langle\langle$ Has-broken-leg, y, **t**; 1 $\rangle\rangle$)[f]).

P is the proposition that the state of affairs which consists of some dog being the object of a, the x-ray in question (at t', the time in question) and that dog's having a broken leg (at the time in question) is factual.

Now that we have seen how to get at the pure information, we want to get at the incremental information that Jackie has a broken leg. We know already that we need the connecting fact that the x-ray was of Jackie. When we consider the incremental information our constraint is simply this: if an x-ray is of this type, and it is the x-ray of a dog, then that dog had a broken leg at the time the x-ray was taken.

The relative constraint is:

$C' = \langle\langle \text{Involves}_R, T, T', T''; 1 \rangle\rangle$

where T, the indicating type is as before. T', the indicated type is

$[s| s \models \langle\langle \text{Has-broken-leg}, \mathbf{y}, \mathbf{t}; 1 \rangle\rangle]$

and T'', the connecting type is:

$[s| s \models \langle\langle \text{Is-xray-of}, \mathbf{x}, \mathbf{y}, \mathbf{t}; 1 \rangle\rangle]$

As before, σ is:

$\langle\langle \text{X-ray}, a, t'; 1 \rangle\rangle \wedge \langle\langle \text{Has-pattern-}\Phi, a, t'; 1 \rangle\rangle$

We assume that σ is factual. Further, we assume that the connecting state of affairs, σ', is factual. Where b is Jackie, σ' is $\langle\langle \text{Is-xray-of}, a, b, t'; 1 \rangle\rangle$.

Any anchor f, such that σ = cond(T)[f] and σ' = cond(T'), must be defined on the parameter **y** of the connecting type, in particular, it must anchor **y** to Jackie.

Thus, for any such anchor f, the proposition carried incrementally by σ relative to C and σ' is the proposition that

$\exists s''(s'' \models \langle\langle \text{Has-broken-leg}, b, t'; 1 \rangle\rangle)$.

Architectural Constraints

As we have seen, sometimes specific information needs incremental information, relative to constraints and connecting facts. There are other ways that can bring about specific information without also involving connecting facts, either via reflexive information or via 'architectural' connecting facts. We will briefly look at some of these ways.

Example 1
In a physician's office thermometers are always shaken down after they are used and stored in a cool place until their next use. One such thermometer (t) is in Elwood's mouth, its mercury is above 98.6.

Given the connecting fact that the thermometer is in Elwood's mouth and the constraint that thermometers indicate that if they are in the mouth of a person and have their mercury above 98.6 that person has a fever, the fact that t has its mercury above 98.6 carries the information that Elwood has a fever. This is the type of incremental information we are familiar with.

Given the constraint that if the mercury in a thermometer goes above 98.6, there is a person whose mouth it has been in and that person has a fever, the signal also carries the reflexive information that there is a person whose mouth t was in and that person has a fever, independent of the connecting fact. That the carrier is itself part of the informational content is why we shall call such information *reflexive*.

Example 2
Consider the apparatus doctors use to check height and weight simultaneously. Elwood is standing on the platform, the weight bars are at 100 and 80, the height bar is at 5ft.

Given the connecting fact that Elwood is the person on the platform, the height bar carries information about Elwood's height, the weight bar about Elwood's weight. Leaving the connecting fact to one side, however, the height bar carries reflexive information about the person whose head it is in contact with and the weight bar about the weight of the person who is affecting it. Given the *architectural connecting fact* that height bar and weight bar are mounted to the same system, and the *architectural constraint* that if a weight bar and a height bar are connected in that way, the person whose head contacts the height bar is the person who is affecting the weight bar, the height bar also carries the *architectural information* that the person affecting the weight bar is 5ft. tall.

In this example we have a case of *coincident architectures*. The weight bar carries information about the person whose head is in contact with the height bar because a certain architectural constraint is in force. However, the original constraints that were sufficient for the reflexive information are independent of the architectural constraint. That the subject matter of the two signal structures (the height bar and the weight bar) is the same, is *induced* by the architecture, not merely reflected by it.

In contrast, *combinative architecture* reflect, rather than induce the relations among contents. Let's have a look at two examples:

Example 3
On the physician's desk are two x-rays, one exhibits property φ, which clearly shows that the person x-rayed had a cracked rib, the other shows a recently mended rib. Both are taken of Elwood at different times. There is nothing in the fact that they are both on the physicians desk that indicates that they are both of the same person. By careful examination, though, the doctor can tell that the mended rib on the one x-ray is the one that is broken on the other.

Example 4
Again two x-rays, both are in a file labelled 'Elwood Fritchey'. Only data about the persons the labels refers to are stored in the files in the doctor's office.

In example 3 we have a type of mere *convergence*. That both x-rays carry information about the same person is due to an internal indication of an external identity but not architectural. That is different in example 4. Here we have a *combinative information system*, a *labelled file*. The architectural constraint is that if a file folder f is labelled a, there is a patient to which a refers, and all of the signals provided by the carriers in f have that patient as subject matter.

Coincident and combinative architectures yield *architecturally co-ordinated information*. To have the complete picture we will briefly look at architecturally mediated information. Information flow, the way we will be interested in, involves such information. In architecturally mediated information signals contain information about a certain subject matter in virtue of carrying information about other signals to which they are architecturally connected. This is an example from Dretske:

> The accoustic waves emanating from a radio speaker carry information about what is happening in the broadcasting studio because they carry accurate information about what is happening in the audio circuit of the receiver; these events in turn carry information about the modulation of the electromagnetic signal arriving at the antenna; and the latter carries information about the manner in which the microphone diaphragm (in the broadcasting studio) is vibrating. The microphone's behavior, in turn, carries information about what the announcer is saying. This whole chain of events constitutes a communication system, a system whose output carries information about its input, because of iterated applications of the xerox principle. (Dretske 1981, 58)

In this story are a lot of signals moving around. There is the sound wave produced by the announcer, the pattern of vibration on the microphone's diaphragm, the electromagnetic signal sent to the antenna, etc. There are constraints and connecting facts for the sound wave to carry the information that the announcer said a certain English sentence. There are architectural constraints and connecting facts that the signal at the antenna can carry the same information, because it additionally carries certain architectural information and certain reflexive information. Each signal in the chain thus carries the information that was produced by the original source, which is why the information goes through. This is the Xerox principle, which we now shall reformulate in the terminology of situation theory:

Definition 4|2-3 (Xerox Principle II)

If s carries the information that b is F, and the fact that b is F carries the information that Q, then s carries the information that Q.

Or more precicely:

> **Definition 4|2–4 (Xerox Principle III)**
>
> If (i) there are architectural constraints C and architectural connections c such that s carries the architectural information that b is F, relative to C given c, and (ii) there are constraints C' and connecting facts c' such that the fact that b is F carries the information that Q relative to C' and c', then there are constraints C" and connecting facts c" such that s carries the information that Q relative to C" given c".

Thus equipped we will now turn to the logic of information flow in the next chapter.

Further Reading
This chapter is based on

- John Perry/David Israel, 'What is information?', in: Philip Hanson (ed.), *Information, Language and Cognition*, Vancouver (University of British Columbia Press) 1990, 1-19.

and

- John Perry/David Israel, 'Information and Architecture', in: J. Barwise et al. (eds.), *Situation Theory and Its Applications, vol. 2*, Stanford University (CSLI) 1991.

5 | Information Flow in Distributed Systems
Renaming Your 'Evening Star' Yields New Information

MCCLEVE put on his wise guy face and confronted Higgins: 'Only the one responsible for the keys of the gardening tools had access to the scythe. And only someone used to gardening could have chopped off the head in a single blow. When I met the old cleaning lady of Pancake Castle she told me that as long as the gardening was done by some of the house's servants instead of outsiders it had been the lower floor butler doing the gardening. As the last one responsible for gardening and mowing you not only had the key but also the knowledge how to use the scythe!'

What does a detective do? Sometimes he looks for persons connected to a crime. Sometimes he already has a list of suspects, and his task is to find out who did it. In a way he *already knows* the culprit, but he does not know her *as* the culprit.

An old fashioned detective (not the one chasing cars and beating it out of people) solves a case by arriving at conclusions that contain the name of the culprit. Conclusions are either linguistic entities if we consider them as the sentences derived, or conclusions may be considered as infons specified by their ontological constituents. But even in the latter case we have access to these conclusions primarily or exclusively by some rendering in language. That makes conclusions relative to a description. The same goes seemingly for the information given by presenting these conclusions. At least arriving at this information requires some reasoning that is done by using language and reasoning along given regularities of a field in question and statements of facts or circumstances.

McCleve knows Higgins. So he knows the culprit, even at the very beginning of his investigations. Knowing her only as Higgins, however, blocks the derivation of the crucial conclusion. Higgins has to be described/classified as the person having the keys to the tools and learned with the scythe. Even after gaining access to the regularity that the servant responsible for the gardening has always been the lower floor butler nothing is gained as long as we not add the further statement that Higgins was the lower floor butler of Pancake Castle at a time when the gardening was still done by some house servant. In deriving at his solution of the case of the gruesome murder in Pancake Castle McCleve had to re-describe the persons involved several times. Renaming/re-describing a person made information/regularities applicable to that person that could not be applied before. Re-description yielded new information, at least in as much as the information could be accessed by McCleve and the authorities taking Higgins away.

Having read the last chapter you surely understood the regularities mentioned as *constraints* linking types of situations. That is correct. And these constraints apply to situation types (respectively sets of infons supported by these situations) and correspondingly to sentences referring to these situations (or the respective infons). The second ingredient we need to be as clever as McCleve are *classification schemes.* A classification scheme provides objects with names and properties. Seeing connections between classification schemes and their properties gives you information.

5 | 1 Information Flow Within the Situation Framework

Information flow requires a logic of distributed systems. If information is said to flow there has to be a system within which it flows. This system has to consist of parts which are separated one way or the other; otherwise there would be no need for information to flow from one part to the other. A system consisting of parts which are separated although constituting a unified whole can be called a 'distributed system'. This chapter deals with one or two simple examples of distributed systems and information flow within them. Jon Barwise and Jerry Seligman developed a formal framework to model information flow. Their book *Information Flow* appeared in 1997. They call the logic involved here the 'Logic of Distributed Systems'. The formal model involves something like constraints, but the formal tools are more abstract than situation theory it is said to have started from. To start with: There are no situations in it!

A Note on Our Presentation: Although all topics are simplified to their core in this course, this applies in the extreme to Barwise and Seligman's theory of information flow. Most details, refinements, some of their ideas on logic and all metalogical properties are left out! The aim of this chapter is to give you an idea of their methods and basic proposals.

Let us begin with some methodological starting points: The analysis should be a *conceptual analysis* or a formal construction of some important conceptual features of information flow (or some concept thereof). We are not looking at what people usually think about information flow or how the mail system is working. We start with some general intuitions about the flow of information and some general principles and tools stemming from analyses of information we have considered so far. The approach is based on principles deemed to be correct. The set of them might be incomplete, but we have to start with some of them to be supplemented in the development of the theory. Examples (like the mail system, printing newspapers, TV, raising the flag etc.) show that modelling real information flow requires many disciplines (logic, cognitive sciences, sociology...). A model of information flow in its own terms tries to arrive at (abstract) laws of information flow. These laws rather reside on a *conceptual* level. The model in its generality covers both physical systems and mathematical proofs!

Information flow is the missing link between justified belief and knowledge. The theory of information flow is related to epistemology, therefore. The theory of information flow follows Dretske in his externalist epistemology: Information flow is a factual concept, not depending on us knowing some conditions being met. Information just flows. Information flow complies, e.g., with the Xerox-Principle.

Remember: It is not an analysis and reconstruction of *all* our present day intuitions.

Distributed Systems

Information flow depends on relationships in a distributed system (e.g., a telephone connection). How the system is carved up is part of the model of the information flow to be explained. What might be a part in one situation/model (e.g., the telephone machine) might be a distributed system of its own in another situation/model. The parts of a distributed system are related to each other by the system as a whole. Regularities ensure the uniform behaviour of the system. What kind of regularities are these? Has the system to be deterministic for information to flow? Deterministic regularities might be the best guarantee for undisturbed information flow – on the other hand most systems, at their usual level of analysis, say an ordinary instruction lesson, are not deterministic systems.

You can see a flashlight as a distributed system in which the parts are connected by being parts of the same system (like in figure 5|1–1).

This diagram tells us nothing about information flow, so far. (We will keep on using the relationships within the parts of a flashlight considered as a distributed system.)

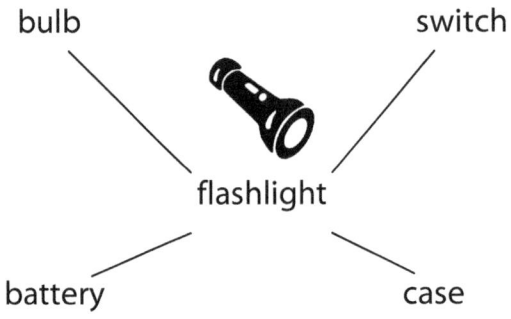

Figure 5|1-1

If you look at examples: the more random a system is the less information will flow. The more random a system is, the more you cannot predict what will happen next in some other part of it. Information flow depends on non-accidental connections, a 'spurious regularity' is not enough. Information flow depends on a *reliable* process. This is a necessary condition of information flow. 'Reliable', however, should not only mean *deterministic* if the model is to fit ordinary distributed system not described in physicalistic language.

Information flow is required to be reliable. That does not mean that it – as might be *reliability* – can be analysed using the concept of causality. The direction of information flow is not necessarily aligned with the direction of causation (you can derive information about the cause from the effect). Informational dependence, therefore, is not causal. In case of loose connections a causal connection might be not sufficient for information flow. So a causal connection is neither necessary for information flow (arriving at information from the effect to its cause) nor sufficient (a loose probable causal connection between two events might not be reliable enough to get information about the second event from information about the first).

Note the connection between information flow and non-randomness (somewhat contrary to the Shannon approach).

Carrying Information

A lot of things are said to *carry* information:

(1) The rifle shot carried the information that the king was dead to the whole city. [The rifle has the property being fired]

(2) The e-mail message bore the information that Albert would be late for dinner. [The message has the property containing the words...]

A common denominator is that in all cases some object having some property matters:

a's being F carries the information that b is G.

We can exploit this observation for a basic idea how to describe distributed systems: Parts of distributed systems are particulars with properties, they are of some type. (Remember the talk about types from Chapter 4|1 on situation semantics' ontology.) Types are connected by constraints. (Remember the definition of constraints in Chapter 4|1.) This is the more obvious if you think of the particulars as situations, although they can as well be any other object you like, and think of the types as infons that are supported by the situations. When the types are connected by some constraint, so are the situations/objects that are of these types respectively. The regularities of a distributed system are represented by the constraints of the complete model of that system as a whole. Information flows along these constraints at the system level (using some local logic, to be explained later).

As a first informal formulation of information flow we get: For a cognitive system x with prior knowledge K a part a of a distributed system being F carries the information that another part b of that system is G if x could legitimately infer from the constraints of the distributed system, given some local logic, that b is G from a is F together with x's prior knowledge K (but not from K alone).

So the cognitive system reasons along the constraints and, given partial knowledge of one end of the system, derives knowledge/information about another part of the system. This reasoning uses a representation not only of the system as a whole but also of the system's parts and their properties. Let us make this more precise.

Classifications

We describe and classify distributed systems and their parts by classifications:

> **Definition 5|1-1**
>
> A *classification* is a structure $A = \langle U, \Sigma_A, \models_A \rangle$ where U is the set of objects to be classified (the tokens of A), Σ_A the set of objects used to classify the tokens (the types of A), and $\models_A$ is a binary relation between U and Σ_A determining which tokens are of which type.
>
> $$a \models_A F$$
>
> says that object a is of the type F given the classification A.

You can think of a as a situation and F as an infon supported by a. Or a may be any kind of object and F a corresponding property. ('Hey, ...' – you might interrupt – '...why then not say 'F(a)' and use First Order Logic?' Good Question. Since we are ultimately interested to use the model also for the support relation between situations and infons or between sets of sentences and derivable consequence we take the more abstract approach of classifications.)

For the purpose of later diagrams we illustrate a classification relation: The classification applies the types in Σ_A to the elements of U, which therefore stand in the relation $\models_A$ to the types.

Sequents

Constraints relate types. We first introduce a more general logical relation:

> **Definition 5|1–2**
>
> Given a classification A a sequent is a pair $\langle \Gamma, \Lambda \rangle$ of sets of types of A. A token a *satisfies* the sequent $\langle \Gamma, \Lambda \rangle$ if
> $(\forall B \in \Gamma)(a \models_A B) \Rightarrow (\exists C \in \Lambda)(a \models_A C)$.

> **Definition 5|1–3**
>
> Γ *entails* Λ in A: $\Gamma \models_A \Lambda$
> if every token of A satisfies $\langle \Gamma, \Lambda \rangle$.

Now we can say what we take a constraint to be.

> **Definition 5|1–4**
>
> If $\Gamma \models_A \Lambda$ then the pair $\langle \Gamma, \Lambda \rangle$ is *a constraint* supported by the classification A.

The constraints of a classification are the sequents that are valid for all the tokens of the classification. Note: In general a constraint is satisfied by a token if the token is of at least one of the types in Λ (Λ is taken disjunctively).

> **Definition 5|1–5**
>
> The set of all constraints supported by A is the *complete theory* of A, Th(A).

Note the following special cases:

Γ, Λ being singletons: 'Γ ⊨$_A$ Λ' means that Γ logically entails Λ in A.

'Γ ⊨$_A$' with right side being empty means in A no token is of type Γ.

'Γ, Λ ⊨$_A$' means, accordingly, that Γ and Λ are mutually exclusive.

'⊨$_A$ Λ, Γ' means that every token of A is of least of one of the types in Λ or Γ.

Infomorphisms

In the first paragraph of this chapter we said that information flows in a distributed system. The system can be considered an information channel. We also said that information flow involves the reliable regularities/constraints that connect parts of the system with each other via the system. This requires mappings from parts to the system as a whole, called 'infomorphisms'. Infomorphism connect classifications.

We are interested in infomorphism that map classifications of parts of a distributed system to the classification of the distributed system itself.

> **Definition 5|1–6**
>
> Let $A = \langle U, \Sigma_A, \vDash_A \rangle$ and $C = \langle V, \Sigma_C, \vDash_C \rangle$ be two classifications. An *infomorphism* between A and C is a pair $f = \langle f^\wedge, f^\vee \rangle$ of functions, such that for all tokens c of C and all types A of A the following (defining statement for infomorphisms) is true:
> $f^\vee(c) \vDash_A A$ iff $c \vDash_C f^\wedge(A)$

What does the defining statement tell us?

We call $f^\vee$ 'f-down' and $f^\wedge$ 'f-up'. The two functions operate in opposite directions: $f: A \rightleftarrows C$. f-down maps *tokens* from the 'right-hand' classification to tokens of the other. f-up maps *types* the other way.

Look again at the defining statement of an infomorphism. Two formulas might express the relations:

(1) Iff the target token (in A) is of some type the token (in C) is of the target type.

(2) The type of the picture is the pictured type of the object.

This might be easier to understand if you look at the following diagram:

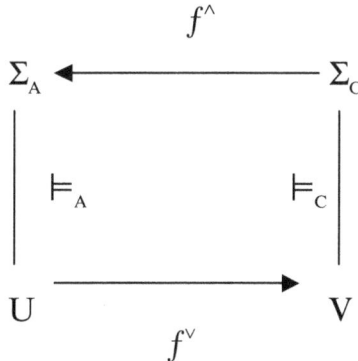

f-down maps the tokens from V to tokens from U, while f-up maps the types from Σ_A to types in Σ_C. What is preserved – and that is expressed by the defining statement of the infomorphism – is the supporting relationship $\models$ in the respective classifications. If there is an infomorphism between two classifications we know that f-down maps a token from V to a token in U that falls under a type in Σ_A if and only if that very type is mapped by f-up to a type in Σ_C that classifies the token we started with in V.

Let us look at an infomorphism example. We are considering our flashlight gain. We are mainly interested in infomorphism that map parts (e.g. a switch) to the whole system (e.g., a flashlight containing a circuit with a bulb).

The classification concerning switches has a set of switches as objects and types that apply to switches. The classification of the whole distributed system contains switches *build into* a circuit and types of these.

If in our theory of (isolated) switches we have a constraint saying 'a pressed switch shows red top'. In our theory of (working) flashlights, which, of course, have switches, we have a constraint saying 'a flashlight with a pressed switch shows red top'. Consider now a switch build into a flashlight. We can map a flashlight (the distributed system) to one of its parts (the switch). Let A be the switch classification and C be the flashlight classification. The flashlight c is mapped by f-down to its switch. And the switch-type *shows-red-top* is mapped by f-up to the flashlight type *has-red-top-shown*. We arrive at a real infomorphism.

Expressed with the fundamental property:

$$\text{the switch} \quad \text{shows red top} \equiv \text{the flashlight} \quad \text{has red top shown}$$
$$f^{\vee}(c) \quad \models_A \quad A \qquad\qquad c \quad \models_C \quad f^{\wedge}(A)$$

Infomorphisms can be added up to make the following diagram commute:

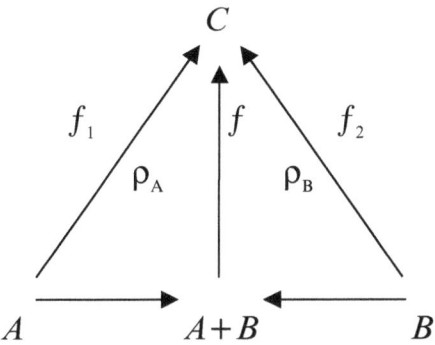

$A+B$ is the sum of the classifications A and B, ρ_A being the projection from A onto $A+B$, so that $\rho_A^\wedge(A) = A_A$ (the A-copy of A), and on tokens $\rho_A^\vee((a, b)) = a$. (Accordingly for ρ_B.) f is the composed infomorphism. f does the same work as the two infomorphism f_1 and f_2 do. While these map isolated parts to a distributed system, f maps pairs (or tuples in case of further addition). This will be of interest, since we want to map all the parts of the system to the system. For this we have to add up all the infomorphisms between the part classifications and the classification of the distributed system. Why do we want to do that? Ultimately we are interested to get information about some distal part of the system from information about some proximal part of the system. The link is established by the distributed system itself *via* the cumulative infomorphism to the parts.

Regularities at System Level

In classifications of parts constraints give us the theory of the (isolated) parts (e.g. bulbs). If parts are built in a distributed system we not only have the sum of the theories of the parts, but regularities that govern the distributed system *as a whole* (e.g., a pressed switch lights the bulb). Such regularities occur only at the system level. These regularities give us information flow. For a system, its classification C and the corresponding theory **Th**(C) (consisting of the constraints for the system as a whole) model them.

The classification of switches A_1 contains a type *Pressed*, the classification of bulbs A_2 contains a type *On*, but they are not related. On the system level there are types corresponding to *Pressed* (say $Pressed_f$) and to *On* (say On_f) which at the system level C are connected by constraints like:

$$Pressed_f \vdash_C On_f$$

If, for example, a flashlight with pressed button has a bulb that is on.

Now we can say what an information channel is:

> **Definition 5|1–7**
>
> An *information channel* consists of an indexed family
> $$C = \{f_i : A_i \rightleftarrows C\}_{i \in I}$$
> of infomorphisms with a common co-domain C, the core of the channel.

The intuition is: the A_i are the (classifications of the) parts of the distributed system C, and it is by virtue of being part of C that tokens of the A_i carry information about one another. Two parts (i.e. tokens of constituent classifications) are connected, if the same token of the co-domain is mapped onto them, i.e. two parts are connected if they are mapped to the same instance of the distributed system.

Example:

A switch s is connected to a bulb b if the infomorphism between the switch classification and the system classification, respectively the co-domain (i.e. the domain of flashlights) maps some flashlight token c to the switch s and the infomorphism between the bulb classification and the system classification maps the very same flashlight c to the bulb b. s and b, therefore, are the switch and bulb of the same flashlight.

Information only flows in the context of a particular token of the co-domain

Information Flow (Outline)

Now we have all ingredients to talk about information flow in a precise way. Suppose, *A* and *B* are constituent/part classifications in an information channel with core *C*. A token *a* of type A in *A* carries the information that a token *b* is of type D in *B* relative to the channel *C* if *a* and *b* are connected in *C* and the translation of A entails the translation of D in Th(*C*).

Once again let us make this clear by looking at our flashlight example. Leaving aside some details – for later –, it may look like this:

B is a bulb classification (with tokens *b*...), *S* is a switch classification, *C* is our classification of working flashlights with tokens *c*... The infomorphism f_1 maps flashlights to bulbs. $f_1^{\vee}(c) = b$ for $c \in W$ (the domain of flashlights). Infomorphism f_2 maps flashlights to switches. $f_2^{\vee}(c) = s$. (That means *b* and *s* are connected in a flashlight *c*.) $f_1^{\wedge}(On) = On_f$ (On_f being a type of flashlights), and $f_2^{\wedge}(Press) = Press_f$ with the constraint holding

$$Press_f \vdash_C On_f$$

and this means nothing else but

$$f_2^{\wedge}(Press) \vdash_C f_1^{\wedge}(On)$$

Press(s) carries the information *On(b)*, since the corresponding types are connected *at the system level*. We have the information that the bulb *b* is on because the switch *s* is pressed, linking two types unlinked before by translating back a constraint valid at the system level (holding for *c*).

To get information about some part of a system, having information about another part, we have to *reason at a distance*. This means: We employ our knowledge about the distributed system and its regularities.

In Detail: We see the part we know about as part of a system, apply some known regularities of the system to this representation of it, derive a system representation of the other part we are looking for, and, finally, translate this back into some simple information about that distant part.

Look at this diagram for reasoning at a distance: Let C be the system, S and B be two constituent classifications with infomorphisms f_1 and f_2:

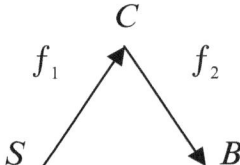

We have to reason – somehow – from S to C and then from C to B, along infomorphisms. To do this, we need some rules of reasoning. These rules allow us to follow or to reverse the work of some infomorphism.

f-Intro and f-Elim

The rules concern mappings of types. Consider an infomorphism between A and C, we reason using these two rules:

f-Intro: $\qquad \dfrac{\Gamma^{-f} \vdash_A \Delta^{-f}}{\Gamma \vdash_C \Delta}$ resp. $\dfrac{\Gamma \vdash_A \Delta}{\Gamma^f \vdash_C \Delta^f}$

Γ^f is the set of translations of Γ, Γ^{-f} the set whose translations are in Γ. Remember that f-up maps types from one classification to another. So if there is a infomorphism f we know that the constraints that hold for types which are mapped by f have still to hold for the types they are mapped on. This is what the right side of the rule f-Intro says. The left side says the same; we only see the types in classification A now as the types we get translating back from types we have in classification C. f-Intro says we can take a valid A-sequent into a valid C-sequent (so map the types).

f-Intro preserves validity: If c were a counterexample to $\Gamma \vdash_C \Delta$, $f(c)=a$ would be a counterexample to $\Gamma^f \vdash_A \Delta^f$.

Example:
If it is valid in A that pressed switches show a red top, it is valid in C that flashlights with their switches pressed have a red top of their switch shown.

f-Intro does not preserve non-validity, since some constraints start with the system level. What is not true for isolated parts may be true for connected parts!

$$f\text{-Elim:} \quad \frac{\Gamma^f \vdash_C \Delta^f}{\Gamma \vdash_A \Delta}$$

f-Elim says we can take a valid C-sequent into a valid A-sequent (so map the types), but f-Elim does *not* preserve validity: There can be a valid constraint $\Gamma^f \vdash_C \Delta^f$ but $\Gamma \vdash_A \Delta$ has a counterexample, although $f(c)$ cannot be a counter-example for any c.

Example:
Flashlights c with pressed switches make light, but some switches a – those not build into flashlights – do not (but they are not connected either. Important for us are the parts that are connected in some system token, so with respect to them we can trust f-Elim). f-Elim preserves non-validity.

We can now use the rules f-Intro and f-Elim for reasoning at a distance. The validity preserving nature of the f-Intro rule tells us that any constraint that holds for a constituent of a system translates to a constraint that holds for the system. And using f-Elim we have that any constraint about the whole system yields a constraint about the components (i.e. those components that are part of a system token).

Let us look back at our example. Consider again the diagram:

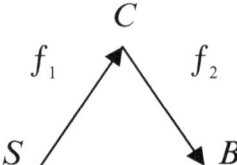

Given the properties of the two rules, we are allowed to reason along the infomorphisms, since validity of constraints concerning *connected* tokens cannot be lost. So if flashlights with pressed switches make light, we know from the switch being pressed that the bulb is on. f-Intro maps the switch type to a type in a relevant system constraint, the right hand side of which is mapped by f–Elim to a bulb type.

Local Logics (Outline)

To make this reasoning precise we need the concept of a local logic, the idea is given by

> **Definition 5|1–8**
>
> A local logic $L = \langle A, \vdash_L, N_L \rangle$ consists of a classification A, a set of sequents, the constraints of L, $\vdash_L$ (satisfying some structural rules [Identity, Weakening, Global Cut]) involving the types of A, and a subset $N_L \subseteq U$ (U being the domain of A), the normal tokens of L, which satisfy $\vdash_L$.

We will not go into the details of the structural rules here. The normal tokens are the connected parts with their distributed system. A local logic L is sound if every token is normal. It is complete if every sequent that holds of all normal tokens is in the consequence relation $\vdash_L$. A sound and complete local logic is a classification with a regular theory (i.e. a theory with the mentioned structural properties).

Reasoning at a distance involves 'moving around' local logics. The inverse of a complete local logic is complete itself.

Given an infomorphism between A and C and a logic L on one of these classifications, we obtain a natural logic on the other. If L is a logic on A, $f[L]$ is the logic on C obtained from L by f-Intro, $f^{-1}[L]$ is the logic on A obtained from a logic L on C by f-Elim. ('$Log_C(A)$' abbreviates such an induced logic.)

Reasoning at a distance in our diagram amounts to:

$$Log_C(B) = f^{-1}[f[Log(A)]]$$

How Information Really Flows

Without going into the meta-logical details of local logics we can say what they are used for: Pushing around local logics means that the sound theory which holds for the distributed systems can be pushed – so to speak – one level down to talk about the parts. Moving around logics is mediated by the channel. (Remember here: infomorphism can be added up, so we need to consider only one classification for all the part classifications, namely the *sum* of all these part classifications.)

Let A be the sum of the constituent classifications, so we have $C \underset{\leftarrow}{\rightarrow} A$.

Given a logic L on the core we use f-Elim to obtain a local logic $f^{-1}[L]$ on A. This logic contains all types of constituents.

Usually, L being scientific, $f^{-1}[L]$ captures information flow from a user's perspective. One could say: The local logic is the 'what' of information flow (what information we are able to derive), the channel is the 'why'.

For the last time let us make this clear in our flashlight example. Let C be again our flashlight classification, B and S be the bulb and switch classifications. We build – remember the diagram for adding infomorphism – a classification $B+S$ and an infomorphism $f = f_1+f_2$, so that for a flashlight token c $f^\vee(c) = (f_1^\vee(c), f_2^\vee(c))$ is the pair of the bulb and the switch of c. Given a type ϕ of C $f^{-1}(\phi)$ is the disjoint union of $f_1^{-1}(\phi)$ and $f_2^{-1}(\phi)$. (Different types of the part classifications can be mapped to the same system type.) If B supports the constraint $\mathit{Lit} \vdash_B \mathit{Live}$, this will be a constraint of $B+S$, since adding the classification preserves their constraints. Then by f-Intro we have a constraint on the system level $f(\mathit{Lit}) \vdash_F f(\mathit{Live})$, F being the local logic of the distributed system. Now F on C supports $\mathit{Illum} \vdash_F \mathit{Elec}$ (emitting photons entails carrying current). We might have as mappings:

$\mathit{Illum} = f(\mathit{Live}) = f_1(\mathit{Live})$, and $\mathit{Elec} = f(\mathit{Press}) = f_2(\mathit{Press})$.

With f-Elim we get:

$\mathit{Lit} \vdash_{B+S} \mathit{Press}$.

Lit is translated back into the part type, since at the system level there is a constraint that continues on $f(\mathit{Lit}) \vdash_F f(\mathit{Live})$. The resulting right hand side *Elec* is translated back into the party type which now is connected by some translation induced constraint to the other part type *Lit*. That is: We know that the switch is pressed, since the bulb is lit – what only holds for pairs that are connected by the same flashlight, these being the *normal* tokens of the logic obtained by applying f-Elim, i.e. $\mathrm{Log}_C(B+S) = f^{-1}[F]$ for the local logic F on C. So what we have done is deriving some 'new' constraints on the sum of the part classifications by translating back constraints of the system level (its local logic). Thereby we have translated talk about parts inasmuch as they are built into the distributed system into talk about the parts. Exploiting the local logic of the distributed system which contains *Illum* and *Elec* we reasoned from the fact that the bulb is lit to the fact that we switched the button. Or we could say: The information that the switch is pressed flows (now) from the fact that the bulb is lit.

We have come a long way. Of course a flashlight is a very simple system, but we hope you have got an idea how we might be able to exploit the constraints governing distributed systems. This is the core of information flow.

Further Reading

The theory of information flow is developed in formal detail in:

- Jon Barwise/ Jerry Seligman, *Information Flow. The Logic of Distributed Systems*, Cambridge (CUP) 1997.

The article

- Jerry Seligman, 'Perspectives in Situation Theory', in: Robin Cooper/Kuniaki Mukai/John Perry (eds.), *Situation Theory and Its Applications*, Stanford 1990, 147-91.

can be considered a precursor containing links to Dretske's theory and to situation semantics, although information flow in *perspectives* does not involve concluding to properties of other tokens, but rather involves a redescription of tokens (namely situations) one already has.

5|2 Information Flow and Paraconsistency

Standard propositional logic contains valid formulas that, intuitively speaking, are hard to accept, for example:

(1)   A true statement is implied by any statement whatsoever.

(2)   A contradiction implies any statement whatsoever.

Or with the conditional junctor '⊃':

(3) $p \supset (q \supset p)$

(4) $p \wedge \neg p \supset q$

The formulas (3) and (4) have been called 'paradoxes of implication', since although they are valid in propositional logic, they run against our pre-theoretic understanding of a conditional. If your cat is on the mat that does not imply – it seems – that Bayern Munich winning their quarter finals against Cologne implies that your cat is on the mat. Whatever the habits of your cat are they are not connected to far remote soccer results. If you happen to hear that Bayern Munich won their quarter final 8:0 and believe – for some mistaken reason – that Cologne also reached the semi-finals you have an inconsistent belief set. Although you do not notice at the moment – say, despite having talked about it only yesterday you do not remember that one of the quarter finals was Bayern Munich against Cologne – *de facto* your belief set is inconsistent. Nevertheless, at that very time you have an inconsistent belief set, you do not deduce any statement whatsoever (e.g. that you can fly right out of your window). Being inconsistent with respect to some facts is not *per se* connected to whatever belief you might have.

There are several varieties of logics which avoid these formulas like (3) and (4) by changing the underlying logic, especially the understanding of the conditional junctor.

Relevant logics are logics that avoid theorems like (3) and (4) by requiring some connection between the antecedent and the consequent of a conditional. A simple truth is not implied by anything, since it does not share content with everything. No true statement shares its content – so it seems – with a contradictory antecedent. One way of requiring the sharing of content is to require that the antecedent and the consequent of a conditional share at least one propositional letter (in the case of a propositional logic – adding quantifiers adds nothing to the problem of the paradoxes of implication). Since the conditional junctor is supposed to capture relations in content (not just truth values) the semantics of conditionals is usually *intensional* (a possible worlds semantics).

Paraconsistent logics in general are logics that allow for the occurrence of some contradiction within a set of formulae without this set (or its set of consequences) becoming trivial, i.e. from the occurrence of some contradiction not any formula can be derived. Deriving for any p both p and $\neg p$ makes a system trivial. Paraconsistent logics accept inconsistency by avoiding triviality. The classical theorem (4) and theorems related to it – for example at least one of those used in the derivation of (4) – have to go. There are several approaches within the field of paraconsistent logic. On the one hand there is a distinction between those who see contradictions as an accident to be avoided, but common enough to have a logic able to deal with them, and those who believe that there really are some true contradictions (i.e. contradictions which will not go away and which can even be proved, say in a system strong enough to express naïve semantics containing its own truth predicate). On the other hand there are distinctions in the formal apparatus or proof theory employed to deal with contradictions. Some systems contain non-standard conjunction, some use constructive implications and some are versions of relevant logics.

Relevant logics come in different systems, there is an American and an Australian tradition. The problem of some relevant logics is not that they do not work from a formal point of view. The problem from a philosophical point of view is that the semantics which is used to show that some systems work and are adequate contains some peculiar truth conditions for negation and implication. If one can avoid the paradoxes of implication only by introducing similarly strange semantic principles or truth conditions, nothing seems to be gained.

What we want to introduce you to in this section is the way in which our picture of information flow from the first section (especially the notion of a channel and a distributed system) might help to dispel some of the doubts one might have concerning the so called *Routley semantics* of relevant logics (named after the pioneer of relevant logics Richard Routley). An interpretation of relevant semantics in the light of information flow might strengthen the relevant approach in logic and support the relevant family of paraconsistent logics. Questions arising from relevant semantics, on the other hand, might lead to refinements in our understanding of information flow.

We give a brief overview of relevant logic and semantics in the Routley tradition with a focus on the truth conditions for conditionals and negation. Information flow enters the picture in reflecting on these conditions. (In our exposition we follow the work of Edwin Mares and Greg Restall. We use 'a', 'b' as variables for possible worlds, 'A', 'B' as schematic letters for any well formed formula and '$\Rightarrow$' as implication in the meta-language.)

Routley Semantics

The requirement that antecedent and consequent share some propositional letter deals with some irrelevant formulas, but (3) will still be around! Furthermore the *variable sharing constraint*, as it is called, does not explain why it holds. Routley's semantics for relevant logics is a version of possible worlds semantics. We have a set of worlds W and within that the *normal* worlds N. Let '$I(A,c)$' mean that for (some) interpretation I the formula A is true at world c. A formula is *valid in a frame* iff it is true on all *normal* worlds on all interpretations. There is an accessibility relation between worlds also, but the crucial difference to standard Kripke semantics is that this accessibility is a ternary relation. Different alethic modal systems put different conditions on the accessibility relation R (like reflexivity, symmetry and so on). Here we start with no condition to hold for R. It does not enter the picture by accounting for '□' (as in most alethic modal logics), but by accounting for the relevant conditional '→'.

So a relevant conditional is taken to be true at some world a if for two other worlds b and c that stand in the accessibility relation to a it is the case that the truth of the antecedent in b brings with it the truth of the consequent in c. Compare the usual truth condition for a modal conditional equivalent to '$\Box(A \supset B)$': In these cases the evaluation of antecedent and consequent is not spread across different worlds; '$\Box(A \supset B)$' is true at some world a iff at all accessible worlds b if the antecedent is true *at b* the consequent is true *at b*.

Since we are free to interpret atomic formula at worlds and the truth condition for the conditional '→' refers to two worlds of evaluation we can have $I(B,b) = true$ and $I(B,c) = false$ thus making even

(5) $A \to (B \to B)$

or – with a similar distribution –

(3') $A \to (B \to A)$

false!

What has this truth condition to do with implication or entailment as we understand it? Is there any interpretation that makes the ternary accessibility relation intelligible? Merely having some truth condition for a conditional junctor that makes some theorems one wants to discard false is in itself no big feat. The semantics given is only a more appropriate semantics for implication or entailment if we can argue that the truth condition introduced is either more natural than the standard one or can at least be given some reading which makes it intelligible and maybe – in connection with the meta-logical results holding for the system – more acceptable.

INFORMATION FLOW AND PARACONSISTENCY

Before we look at an interpretation from the point of view of information flow, let us first show that by some further conditions on accessibility in frames '→' can be tied to our informal notion of entailment. We can define

> **Definition 5|2–1**
>
> A entails B iff $(\forall w \in W)(I(A, w) = true \Rightarrow I(B, w) = true)$.

Entailment in this sense means 'implies in all possible worlds'. Note that the evaluation of antecedent and consequent is done at the same world (as one should expect). To capture entailment, a reflexive and transitive relation $\leq$ on the worlds is introduced:

> **Definition 5|2–2**
>
> $(\forall a, b \in W)(a \leq b \Leftrightarrow (\exists n \in N) R(n, a, b))$

Two worlds stand in the relation $\leq$ iff there is a normal world which connects the two in its ternary accessibility. (This again has no obvious intuitive reading.) Further on one requires a *heredity fact*

(6) $(\forall a, b \in W)(I(A, a) = true \land a \leq b \Rightarrow I(A, b) = true)$

So truths are inherited from a world a to all $\leq$-related worlds b. Given our truth condition for '→' we can define *normal implication*:

> **Definition 5|2–3**
>
> ---
>
> A normally implies $B \Leftrightarrow (\forall n \in N)(I(A \rightarrow B, n) = \text{true})$.

This is just relevant implication in the normal worlds. Interestingly enough now one can prove an important meta-logical theorem:

> **Theorem 5|2–1**
>
> ---
>
> A entails $B \Leftrightarrow$ A normally implies B

Theorem 5|2–1 tells us that in the normal worlds our intuitively acceptable notion of entailment is mirrored by relevant implication. This is a big step towards justifying the intuitive soundness of the relevant conditional '$\rightarrow$' and its ternary accessibility relation. The right to left direction tells us that we do not introduce new implications by our ternary accessibility. Since R gives us more possibilities to falsify formulas this may be no big surprise. The left to right direction of Theorem 5|2–1 tells us that the normal worlds are complete with respect to entailments. (Note that 'A' does not *entail* '$B \rightarrow B$' either, since the latter does not hold at all worlds, as we have seen above.) *Normal worlds* are – at least in some of the system of relevant logic – those worlds which satisfy the principle of excluded middle and which are consistent. Since relevant logic is paraconsistent there are plenty of worlds which do not meet these conditions.

We still do not know, however, how we should understand the ternary relation. That is where the perspective of information flow comes into the picture (in the next subsection).

Before we look at that we have to look at the semantics of negation, the second major deviation from standard logic, and the second major stumbling block for anyone trying to understand relevant semantics.

Negation gets its non-standard treatment by the (in)famous *Routley star* '*'. For any world w there is postulated a *witness world* w^*.

> **Truth Condition** ¬
>
> ---
>
> $I(\neg A, a) = true$ iff $I(A, a^*) = false$

Once again the evaluation is spread across two worlds. Note that the truth condition only requires that '$\neg A$' is true at a world a iff A is false at a^*; nothing is said whether the behaviour of 'A' at a depends on what is the case at a^*. So we can have $I(A,a) = true$, $I(A,a^*) = I(B,a) = false$, giving us that

(4') $A \wedge \neg A \rightarrow B$

turns out *false*. a in this case is a world where A and $\neg A$ both are *true* (showing that this semantics is paraconsistent).

Given its truth condition, however, '¬' seems to be something completely different from standard negation. What is a witness world, anyway? A couple of logicians accustomed to the construction of formal semantics have complained that this goes to far, that one gets no idea what this truth conditions is supposed to tell us (e.g., van Bentham 1979).

The Information Flow Perspective

As we saw in Chapter 5|1, information flows in a distributed system, which can be considered the channel along which we reason. Talking in situation semantics language we can say that information about one situation is derived from another situation by some channel. Situations were introduced as parts of reality. The channel is also a part of reality (trivially so if we see the distributed system as a channel). Therefore there is a situation that comprises exactly the channel. The infons made factual by that situation are the infons that describe the structure of the channel. The important thing is: The channel as well as the parts (be it two or more) are situations and can be relata of a ternary relation connecting entities of some type. The channel and two sites connected by a channel can be seen as the relata of the ternary accessibility relation R. Look again at the truth condition of '$\rightarrow$': The relation that is said to hold between b and c is established or observed from a. Let a be the channel and b and c be the sites connected by the channel. We can say that the channel establishes the connection between the sites, and from the perspective of the distributed system the sites are relata of information flow. '$A \rightarrow B$' receives the following interpretation: '$A \rightarrow B$' is true at a if all the sites/situations b and c connected by that channel are such that if the information A is available at the one end b, the information B is available in situation c. The more constraints hold for a distributed system *the less* situations can be derived from it, since the derived situations have to meet all the constraints. Having more constraints operative in a channel means zooming in on a very specific part/situation.

This amounts to an interpretation of a ternary accessibility relation in terms of information flow. And it allows us to introduce a second reading of '$\rightarrow$'. (The first reading of '$\rightarrow$' – expressed by Theorem 5|2–1 – was 'entailment in the normal worlds'.) The second reading of '$\rightarrow$' says:

> $\rightarrow$ Reading 2
>
> ---
>
> '$A \rightarrow B$' is true with respect to a channel c iff '$\{A\} \vdash_c \{B\}$' is a constraint for that channel c.

To spell this reading out there should be infomorphisms mapping what is said in '*A*' and '*B*' at the system level to statements/infons of the part classifications (cf. Chapter 5|1). An interpretation also has to be developed for the equivalent of the occurrence of nested arrows '→'. It seems that one has to allow constraints that constrain lower level constraints.

Edwin Mares gives a further interpretation of '→' in terms of situations and information flow exploiting the fact that an infon (made true by some situation) can contain information about situations (i.e. can contain parameters or constants for situations). An infon can contain information about relations between infons and situations. Infons of this kind are *informational links*. They tell us that some infon being factual *involves* a second infon being factual (see Chapter 4|2 on information architecture). An informational link has the form: $\langle\langle involves, \Phi, \Psi, 1\rangle\rangle$ where Φ and Ψ are situation types. These types are introduced by abstraction on situations supporting infons (see Chapter 4|1). Say we have the following two type definitions using a situation parameter 's*':

$$\Phi = [s^* \mid s^* \vDash \phi]$$

$$\Psi = [s^* \mid s^* \vDash \varphi]$$

that is φ and ϕ are the infons the support of which defines the type. They give the informational content associated with the types. One can take the ternary accessibility relation R to represent these informational links. If some informational link is said to hold in situation *a* saying that an infon ϕ carries the information that the infon φ also has to hold (somewhere), then if $R(a, b, c)$ and *b* contains/supports the infon ϕ, then *c* contains/supports the infon φ. The ternary relation models an informational link of one situation/infon constraining another. We arrive at:

> → Reading 3
>
> 'A → B' is true with respect to situations a, b, c such that $R(a,b,c)$ if it is true that if $a \vDash \langle\langle \mathit{involves}, \Phi, \Psi, 1\rangle\rangle$ and $b \vDash \phi$, then $c \vDash \varphi$.

This reading is substantially the same as reading 2: Whereas the latter models the truth condition of '→' by the formalization of constraints and the theory of a distributed system this reading treats constraints by the *involves* relation that is part of the informational architecture. If we take R to be about or related to informational links some features of information linkage should be mirrored by the relation R. Every situation is closed under informational linkage, since information is factual: given that some piece of information is present in a situation and is linked to some other piece of information the second piece is already there, just as information is out there in the world. The involved information needs not to be linked to the situation by a special act or discovery, it is simply there. This means for relation R that one should require it to be reflexive:

(7) $R(a,a,a)$

If a contains an information link, (7) guarantees the closure of it with respect to a. The set of statements made true by a is then closed under *modus ponens*. Note that (7) does not make obvious sense, however, in the second reading of '→': Not every channel carries information from itself to itself! On the other hand (7) seems vacuously true on the second reading, since the information present in the system is present in the system (as its own improper part) if it is present in the system (as its own improper part).

What about negation?

If the situation framework could deal with the '*'-operator as well, it might well become the preferred reading of relevant truth conditions.

A piece of information can be incompatible with another piece of information. This may be due to the polarities within the infons supported by the situation or due to constraints yielding implied information of the one infon incompatible with the other. Suppose we had made this intuition more precise and given a formal account of compatibility, say by using infon logic or by considering metalogical properties of the theories of distributed systems (i.e. their set of supported constraints). We could then introduce a relation $C(a, b)$ of compatibility between situations or the sets of infons supported by these situations. The statement $\neg A$ is true at a, then, if the truth of A is incompatible with the other information contained in a related situation b. The closure of a situation can be taken as what the situation says. The set of compatible situations can be taken as that which is not excluded by what the situation says. If the negation of some state of affairs A is a fact in all a compatible situations, the state of affairs is not compatible with a, so presumably its negation is contained within what a says. $a*$ (the witness world referred to in the explanation of the Routley star) can be taken as the maximal situation such that the information given in a is compatible with it.

We arrive at a

> ¬ Reading
>
> ---
>
> $I(\neg A, a) = true$ iff for all b such that $C(a, b)$, $I(A, b) = false$.

That is, a negation is true in a situation a if in all other situations compatible with the information given in a the statement under consideration is false. $a*$ just is the most informative (since most comprehensive) of these situations. Not every situation is compatible with itself, since we assumed that there are inconsistent situations.

These kinds of truth conditions of '$\rightarrow$' and '$\neg$' refer the evaluation of some formula from some situation at which it is to be evaluated to *another* situation. Especially the truth condition for relevant implication does not require that the information linked to the information given in situation *a* is completely present in *a* itself. This is as it should be in situation semantics, since we are interested in partiality. Infon logic requires a few conditions of minimal logical closure of infons supported by some situation. Closure under *modus ponens* (i.e. a corresponding principle for infons, not statements) may be part of (an) infon logic. We would, however, give away the whole idea of partiality if all information that is somehow linked has to be present in that very situation. Requiring this would take us back to worlds (if there are no informationally isolated parts of worlds).

A Relevant Logic

We will not go into the details of the various relevant logical systems and their distinctions here, but for the curious we present just one system of relevant logic that is sound and complete with respect to a reading from the information flow perspective.

The system **E** is a basic system of relevant logic, considered to capture the notion of entailment (therefore the name '**E**'):

1    $A \rightarrow A$

2    $(A \wedge B) \rightarrow A$

3    $(A \wedge B) \rightarrow B$

4    $((A \rightarrow B) \wedge (A \rightarrow C)) \rightarrow (A \rightarrow (B \wedge C))$

5    $((A \rightarrow C) \wedge (B \rightarrow C)) \rightarrow ((A \vee B) \rightarrow C)$

6   $A \to (A \vee B)$

7   $B \to (A \vee B)$

8   $(A \wedge (B \vee C)) \to ((A \wedge B) \vee (A \wedge C))$

9   $\neg\neg A \to A$

10 $(A \to B) \to ((B \to C) \to (A \to C))$

11 $(A \to (A \to B)) \to (A \to B)$

12 $(A \to \neg B) \to (B \to \neg A)$

13 $(A \to \neg A) \to \neg A$

14 $(((A \to A) \wedge (B \to B)) \to C) \to C$

As rules **E** contains:

(i) $\vdash A \to B, \vdash A \Rightarrow \vdash B$

(ii) $\vdash A, \vdash B \Rightarrow \vdash (A \wedge B)$

We give only the propositional part, since that is the level where the considerations of relevance come in (just as in paraconsistent logics), one may add standard modal quantification theory. Interestingly enough it can be proved that even the propositional part of a relevant logic like **E** is not decidable! Greg Restall develops a semantics of situation frame structures in the vain of the second reading of '$\to$' which invalidates some the theorems of **E**, but is decidable.

Further Reading

The whole section is based on work of Edwin Mares and Greg Restall, see:

- Edwin Mares, 'Relevant Logic and the Theory of Information', *Synthese* 109 (1996), 345-60.

- Edwin Mares/Robert Meyer, 'Relevant Logics', in: Lou Goble (ed.), *Philosophical Logic*, Oxford 2001, 280-308.

- Greg Restall, 'Information Flow and Relevant Logics', in: Jerry Seligmann/Dag Westerstahl, (eds.), *Logic, Language and Computation*, Stanford 1996, 463-77.

You can find the different systems of relevant logics and their metatheory in the textbooks

- Richard Routley et. al., *Relevant Logics and Their Rivals*, Atascadero 1982.

- Steven Read, *Relevant Logic*, Oxford 1988.

A textbook length introduction to the philosophical questions and formal systems of paraconsistent logics – unfortunately in German – is:

- Manuel Bremer, *Wahre Widersprüche. Einführung in die parakonsistente Logik*, Sankt Augustin 1998.

An earlier, similar overview is given by the introductions written by Richard Routley and Graham Priest in the volume:

- Graham Priest/Richard Routley/Jean Norman (eds.), *Paraconsistent Logic. Essays on the Inconsistent*, Munich 1989.

see also for an overview focussing on relevant varieties:

📖 Graham Priest, 'Paraconsistent Logic', in: D. Gabbay/F. Günthner (eds.), *Handbook of Philosophical Logic*, 2nd Edition, Dordrecht 2000.

5|3   Get Yourself Involved into Impossible Situations

Sometimes people say things like 'You put me in an impossible situation.' or 'That put me in an impossible situation.' What they usually mean by that is not that they are or were in circumstances which falsified the laws of logic, but rather that the situation they are or were in was pretty unpleasant. Anyway, in this chapter we shall look at situations in the way we have introduced it as a technical term and consider the incentives to say about some of them that they are impossible, literally speaking, but nevertheless *are*.

At first sight, this doesn't seem to raise a substantial problem, does it? You might wonder why anybody should bother whether or not there should be impossible situations. At least there clearly seem to be possible situations, for all actual situations are clearly possible situations. So why shouldn't we also assume that besides the actual situations, there are the possible situation (some of which are mere possible situation, viz. those which are not actual) and finally the impossible situations. If it makes sense to say that some situations are possible, it should also make sense to say that some situations are impossible. Sounds like some existential commitment being involved, so why not assume that there are impossible situations?

Well, one way to argue against this line of thought could be that it parallels Meinong's reasoning for the being of non-existing objects (or what Quine called the 'platonic riddle of nonbeing'). Some things don't exist. Prime examples for this are Santa Clause, unicorns, elves. But what is it of which we truly claim that it does not exist? If there are things that don't exist, then they *are*. Thus besides the existing things there are also the non-existing things. These are the things we can truly say of that they don't exist. Just as most philosophers do not like this reasoning to much, for it overcrowds the ontology with all sorts of dumb things, philosophers with taste for desert landscapes, do not like impossible situations much. It's already weird enough to assume that there are more situations than the actual ones, it would be better to avoid situations which are not only not located in space and time, but moreover not even representable by a coherent description (as the possible situations presumably are).

In this chapter we will discuss arguments why possible situations and even impossible situations are a welcome enrichment for the theory of information flow we discussed throughout the book. Moreover, we will learn how information theory can be exploited to explicate the notion of possibility and necessity. To get started, we shall first try to get a little bit clearer on what *possible* situations are and then consider impossible ones.

From Possible Worlds to Possible Situations

As we have seen from the very beginning of the book, information was always said to be analyzable, at least in part, in terms of excluded possibilities. Since Carnap's and Bar-Hillel's theory of semantic information we tried to express this intuition more rigidly in a theory which quantified over possible worlds. When we discussed possible worlds in that chapter, we followed Carnap's notion of a possible world, or 'state description', which was defined as a certain class of sentences:

> A class of sentences [in a language-system], which contains for every atomic sentence either this sentence or its negation, but not both, and no other sentences, is called a state-description [in the language system], because it obviously gives a complete description of a possible state of the universe of individuals with respect to all properties and relations expressed by predicates of the system. (Carnap 1947, 9)

Thus we have dealt with possible worlds as being linguistic constructions. There are reasons to favor another notion of possible worlds, reasons which are somewhat related with the kind of realism which is typical for situation semantics. To get there, we shall first explore an extreme form of realism.

David Lewis is famous for defending what we will call 'modal realism' (Lewis 1986), according to which the possible worlds we quantify over in the theory of probability or in formal semantics are all pretty much like our world. In fact our world is just one world among many, which are spatiotemporally isolated from each other and which don't bear causal relations. What happens in these possible worlds is independent from our language. There might be more possible properties than we have predicates and more possible individuals than we have names for, or that exist in our world. All these possible worlds are concrete; they exist in the way our world exists, with the minor difference that our world is actual, whereas the others are not. Since these worlds are pretty much like our world, each of them is wholly determinate. There might, for example, be numerous possible worlds in which I am walking down the beach in St. Andrews right now but which all differ in some other respect, for example with respect to who is the current vice-president of the first pigeon breeding society of the village of Düsseldorf-Rath.

To assume such a manifold of possible worlds is for a number of reasons too much to swallow for some philosophers. One reason is that it seems to overcrowd our ontology with the weirdest objects, possible worlds, all as real as the one we happen to inhabit, but wholly isolated from us and all kinds of possible individuals living there. Another reason is that although extreme modal realism provides a straightforward solution for the semantical analysis of our modal talk (it is straightforward, since we can take the paraphrases of modal logic at face value), it nevertheless betrays epistemology. We know that some things are possible, some things are necessary and some are neither, but if we have no causal contact with the facts that make our modal believes true, it seems mysterious how we ever could have acquired such knowledge. Such a tension between the solution for the semantics of a certain domain and the epistemology of that domain (mathematics and ethics are two other such domains), is generally called a *Benacerraf-problem*, named after Paul Benacerraf who formulated it for mathematics. This is how O'Leary-Hawthorne has put it for modalities:

> Assume that our modal talk and thought is not really committed to the existence of possibilia, possible worlds, ways things might have been. A puzzle naturally arises. How are we now to explain away the apparent reference to such modal entities in our everyday talk about the space of possibility [...]? Assume instead that our modal talk and thought is genuinely committed to the existence of possibilia. Now an epistemological problem looms large.

> How do we know that the entities we purport to refer to exist and how do we know what they are like? As we make the epistemological problem tractable we face an apparently intractable semantic problem. As we make the semantic problem tractable, we face an apparently intractable epistemological problem. (O'Leary-Hawthorne 1996, 183)

If such tension seems to be dragging us to unattractive extremes, it might be best to steer middle course.

Like Lewis, Barwise will assume that there are ways things might have been. But what is the actual complement to the way things might have been? It is not 'I and my surroundings' as Lewis suggests, such that other mere possible worlds are just like that, but rather *the way things are*, a property or state of the world, not the world itself. We will take these ways things might have been as real, but although they are real, they are neither concrete nor isolated from the actual world. Just as everything that exists at all, these ways the world might have been are elements of the actual world, they are abstract objects, abstracted from the activities of rational agents and – in this sense – they depend on these activities. Robert Stalnaker, who suggested this view of possibilities, calls it 'moderate modal realism'.

One might wonder how much of a realism this in fact is. If the dependence of the ways things might have been is *ontological* dependence, such that the way things might have been exist only as the contents of considerings of rational agents (as Stalnaker seems to suggest), their existence is clearly mind-dependent. For epistemic contexts this might be enough realism. And since we are dealing with information, which is an epistemic notion, one might argue that this is all we need as an account of possibilities for our purposes, but let's see.

The abstractions, moderate modal realism considers, diverge in several respects from the possible worlds Lewis is talking about. It is crucial to get clear of this difference to understand how we will be able to model informational contexts with their help. To mark the difference between possible worlds and the abstractions we consider, we shall call ours *possible states*. This is – as we will see in a minute – anyway more appropriate. Now, in what respects do they differ from hardcore possible worlds? We will try to explain it a little with an analogy we borrow from Barwise.

Consider a fairly simple card game. Two players, we will call them Max and Claire, each get one card from a deck of cards of denominations, K (king), Q (queen), and J (jack). The relative ranking of the cards is $K > Q > J$, and the player who was given the higher card wins (if they should be given cards of the same denomination, the play results in a draw). Let's suppose first that the two players play the game sufficiently often, say 10,000 times, and destroy the deck after these 10,000 hands.

If we interpret instead each hand as a possibility in the extreme modal realist's sense, Max and Claire play the game in a number of possible worlds, of which there are 10,000. Although Max and Clare might have identical cards in their hands in quite a number of these possible worlds, all these hands (or possible worlds) differ, for they are taking place at different times and different places. Each present hand is the actual hand, and all 9,999 past or future hands are the other possible hands. (Thus we draw a temporal analogy to possibilia. What is present, is actual.)

If, on the other hand, we take a moderate perspective on the matter, there are nine possible relevant states these hands can be in, namely:

$$\langle K, K \rangle, \langle K, Q \rangle, \langle K, J \rangle, \langle Q, K \rangle, \langle Q, Q \rangle, \langle Q, J \rangle, \langle J, K \rangle, \langle J, Q \rangle, \langle J, J \rangle$$

A given hand is thus an ordered pair, such that a hand h is in state $\langle K, J \rangle$ if in h Max has a K and Claire has a J.

Now consider the proposition which is expressed by

(1)   Claire has a Q.

If we adopt the perspective of extreme modal realism, this proposition will be modeled by the set p of all possible worlds (of all hands), in which Claire happens to have a Q. It will be true for some specific hand h iff $h \in p$. If Claire has a Q in all 10,000 hands, the proposition expressed by (1) will be deemed necessary, if she never has a Q (and p is empty), it will be deemed impossible and otherwise contingent.

If, on the other hand, we take the perspective of the moderate approach, the proposition expressed by (1) is modeled by the following set p^*:

$$\{\langle K, Q\rangle, \langle Q, Q\rangle, \langle J, Q\rangle\}$$

The modal status of the proposition is then determined by the possibility of the nine states we started with. If, e.g., all these states are possible states, then the proposition expressed by (1) will be contingent, for p^* contains some but not all of the possible states.

That we model the proposition expressed by (1) with p^* rather than with p introduces a certain relativity or certain form of pragmatism into our analysis. The 'right set of all possibilities' is on the extreme view a brute modal fact, it is simply an issue of how many possible worlds there are in which Max and Claire play the game. On the moderate view, we selected only those states which were relevant for determining the winner of the game, according to its rules. The nine possible states we consider don't keep track of different suits of the cards or what Claire and Max had for breakfast at the day of the play. These questions are not at issue in the game, thus we didn't keep track of them. Possible states are, just the way we introduced situation in the very beginning, not complete universes in which everything is settled one way or other, but rather equivalence classes of such worlds in which what is settled depends on what is at issue.

In fact, pragmatism enters our moderate view at two stages. One pragmatic factor is the question of what is at issue, or – if we frame it in epistemic terms – :

(i)   What issues are relevant to the given enquiry?

(i) is determined by what one wants to know or to find out. In the simple card game, what was at issue was only the denomination of the card; does it have a Q, a K, or a J on it? Let's make the case a little more complicated and assume that not only the denomination matters, but also the suit of the card, and that instead of the jack, we play the game with the joker (it's still called *J*, and we will treat it just like the jack in our ranking). For simplicity, we shall assume that there are only two suits, ♠ and ♣. ♠ > ♣, which is introduced as a rule of the game, e.g., for the case in which the game results in a draw. Given what is relevant to determine the winner of each hand, we get the following states (we use obvious abbreviations here):

⟨K♣, K♠⟩, ⟨K♣, K♣⟩, ⟨K♠, K♣⟩, ⟨K♠, K♠⟩, ⟨K, Q⟩, ⟨K, J⟩, ⟨Q, K⟩, ⟨Q♣, Q♠⟩, ⟨Q♣, Q♣⟩, ⟨Q♠, Q♣⟩, ⟨Q♠, Q♠⟩, ⟨Q, J⟩, ⟨J, K⟩, ⟨J, Q⟩, ⟨J♣, J♠⟩, ⟨J♣, J♣⟩, ⟨J♠, J♣⟩, ⟨J♠, J♠⟩

Again, pragmatically, we didn't consider the states irrelevant according to the rules of the game. Now, consider the proposition expressed by (2):

(2)   Max has a higher card than Claire, and both have a *J*.

According to the rules of the game and our moderate view, this proposition is modeled by the following singleton set p^{**}:

(p^{**}) {⟨J♠, J♣⟩}

p^{**} is a way to solve all the issues which are relevant for determining that Max is the winner and that both have a *J*. But is this way of resolving all the issues a *possible* state? We might deem it to be a possible state, for we might be ignorant of the fact that jokers don't have a suit. If this information is revealed to us, the state in p^{**} is revealed not to be a possible state. It is information about the relevant states which makes some of them possible and some of them not. (2) expresses an impossible proposition. Thus, the second pragmatic aspect of our view enters through the following question:

(ii)   What information is currently available concerning these issues?

It often depends on the context what states are considered possible and what states are not considered possible. Have a look at the following arguments:

A1
- The morning star is the brightest heavenly body in the morning sky.
- ∴ The evening star is the brightest heavenly body in the morning sky.

A2
- This apple is green all over.
- ∴ This apple is not red all over

A3
- All men are mortal and Socrates is a man.
- ∴ Socrates is mortal.

A4
- Justin is a human being.
- ∴ Justin isn't taller than 9 ft.

If we are to judge the validity of A1-4, we will usually turn to some logical system, give a regimentation of the premise and the conclusion and either try to find a proof of the conclusion from the premise or a counterexample. A counterexample, quite generally, is an instantiation of the same argument pattern, for which the premises are clearly true and the conclusion clearly false. If we can accomplish this task, and find such an instantiation into the argument pattern, we can conclude that the argument is not valid (and thus not sound). Why is that so?

The idea is that the validity of an argument depends on the holding of the logical consequence relation between the premises and the conclusion. Logical consequence holds if it is *not possible* that the premises are true, but the conclusion is false. A counterexample, on the other hand, shows that this modal connection does in fact not hold – it is possible that the premises are true, although the conclusion is false.

Those of you that have taken a course in First Order Logic already might be familiar with argument A3. If we regiment the inference pattern in FOL, we get the following valid argument:

A3* $\forall x\,(Man(x) \rightarrow Mortal(x)) \wedge Man(socrates)$

∴ $Mortal(socrates)$

In FOL we can give a proof that this argument is valid, and there is no way to find an instantiation of the argument pattern

A3** $\forall x\,(F(x) \rightarrow G(x)) \wedge F(a)$

∴ $G(a)$

such that the premise is true, but the conclusion is false. For all other arguments given above things are less clear. In fact you might think that A3 is actually the only valid argument. But if you check back with the notion of validity we used, and the definition of logical consequence we gave, all of these arguments should turn out valid. It is for none of them the case that the premise could be true, but the conclusion false. It is just *not possible* that this could be the case. Men are never taller than 9 ft. (the tallest man was Bob Pershing Wadlow from Alton, Illinois, who was excatly 8ft. 11 in. when measured for the last time in 1940), nothing which is in one color all over could be in some other color all over the same time, and Venus could not possibly be distinct from itself.

Some of you might want to object 'But wait, there are several different notions of possibility conflated here. The definition of logical consequence meant logical possibility, whereas the modalities we are speaking of, e.g., in A4 are natural at best.'

True, if the context in which you have to evaluate the validity of A1-A4 is a logic course, the context determines that you should better be concerned with logical possibilities. Evaluating it impossible that one object could be green all over and red all over the same time, and thus judging A2 to be valid will be a mistake if the context is First Order Logic. Only if more information is made available, e.g., if a broader sense of logical consequence is the subject under scrutiny and meaning postulates are added to the information that counts as available, it will be impossible that such an object could exist.

The same holds for Justin's height. Even *with* meaning postulates it is still possible that Justin could be taller than 9 ft., thus the conclusion of A4 is certainly not logically entailed in the premise. In the context of a logic class, or a metaphysical discussion, people over 9ft. tall might count as a relevant possibility, but if the context is the construction of door frames for a house in which Justin is supposed to live in, other modalities begin to matter, and it ceases to be possible that Justin is taller than 9 ft.

The different contexts here are the different contexts in which A1-4 are considered valid arguments even by individuals who have the same information at their disposal. You probably know that men cannot be taller than 9 ft., but you should better not consider this to be available information when at the end of Baby Logic the exam question is to tell whether or not A4 is a valid argument.

When you were still a small kid, without much knowledge about the average height of people, being yourself so small that almost everybody looked like being more than 9ft. tall to you anyway, the information that is at your disposal nowadays, was not at your disposal back then. This is another way how context determines what a relevant possibility is and what is not. It is determined by what information is *de facto* available to an agent. This is what we call *epistemic availability*.

A variant of epistemic availability is *doxastic availability*. Here we consider not what an agent *knows*, but what an agent *believes*. An agent might deem states impossible (because of having false beliefs) which may in fact be impossible. It is mainly for matters of epistemic and doxastic availability that we are interested in impossible states. To this we shall now turn.

Impossible States and the Granularity Problem

One of the questions repeatedly raised throughout the book was the question of how to get at the informational content of logical truths. We have considered various alternative solutions to it, which we all found wanting so far. Let's remind ourselves what the problem was.

Jon Barwise has a nice example of somebody who gets dressed to go out and is faced with tying his shoes. Which shoe shall he tie first? What he obviously can't do is to tie each shoe first. It doesn't seem to be possible to do two distinct things and each before the other. Now if we look at the proposition which is said to be impossible, viz. that somebody can tie each of his shoes before the other, and ask ourselves how it would adequately be modeled in the possible worlds framework, we remember from the chapters before that we would have to model it with the empty set of possible worlds. Since the proposition is an impossibility, there are no worlds compatible with it.

Now, as we noted already, this is the same as the set which models the proposition that $2+2 = 5$, the set in which Fermat's last theorem is false. Given the possible worlds framework very different claims are modeled as expressing the same proposition. This seems clearly false, since then doubting or believing or claiming one of these should be the same as doubting or believing or claiming one of the others, which it isn't. This is what is called 'the granularity problem'. The trouble is that the possible worlds framework alone is not able to represent propositions fine-grained enough to catch crucial differences.

Informationalism now tries to model these crucial differences with the help of logically impossible states. We will have a look at one example that models a logical 'inquiry', to see where the logical impossibilities enter. The example is, again, from Barwise.

Let us suppose that the relevant issues of an inquiry include whether some domain M satisfies the first-order sentence θ as well as first-order sentences $\varphi_1, ..., \varphi_N$, and that it is already established that each φ_i is not the case. In other words, each $M \vDash \neg \varphi_i$ is included in the available information. Let us further suppose that the sentence

(S) $\theta \vee \varphi_1 \vee ... \vee \varphi_N$

is a theorem of first-order logic. The fact that M satisfies S may not be included in the available information, and even if it is there is no reason to suppose that $M \vDash \theta$ is included in the available information, even though it is a logical consequence of the available information. For example if we are dealing with epistemic possibility and N is very large, the agent may not realize that the set $\{\varphi_i \mid i = 1 \ldots N\}$ exhausts the remaining disjuncts of (S). Checking that this is so is a step that must be gone through before $M \vDash \theta$ becomes available. Until this, our (epistemically) possible states include the (logically impossible) states where $M \vDash \neg \theta$ is the case alongside each of $M \vDash \neg \varphi_i$. This is a state that could not be modeled with the help of the standard possible worlds framework, because this state is not a logically possible state. But, although this state is logically impossible, it is epistemically possible and thus a state we want to keep track of. Here are some of the core features of this pragmatic theory of possibility as developed by Barwise (given in the form of partial explications rather than definitions):

Issues
The set of all states of a given inquiry depends on the system under investigation and on the issues regarding the system relevant to the inquiry.

States
A state is a way of resolving all the relevant issues.

Impossibilities
The set of possible states at a given point in the inquiry depends on the information concerning the issues currently available. The impossible states are those incompatible with the currently *available* information; the others are possible.

Available Information
What information is available at any given point in an inquiry is a context-sensitive matter, depending on the kind of possibility one is considering and on the progress of the inquiry up to that point.

Increases in information
The correct elimination of any nonempty set of possibilities corresponds to a strict increase in the information available at the next stage in the investigation.

Decrease in possibilities
Conversely, the acquisition of any new information corresponds to a strict decrease in the states that are possible.

Given this pragmatic theory of possibility, especially the fact that informationally relevant states are added to the mere logically possible states, *knowledge* of necessities does not anymore collapse into *belief* in necessities (a problem we had in Dretske's original account).

Given that you know that Paul is bald, seeing Paul being bald does not add anything to your knowledge, although it does to mine, being previously ignorant of Paul's tragic fate. Receiving a signal stating that (S) is a theorem of first-order logic might, again, not add anything to your knowledge and thus might not be of informational value for you, but it might contain information for me, because

(S') $\quad \neg(\theta \vee \varphi_1 \vee ... \vee \varphi_N)$

might be an epistemic possibility among the states that model my logical ignorance. As you can see, the receiver plays a much bigger role here in determining what a signal can inform him about than in our previous models.

But this change in the theory seems to be quite natural. Consider Dretske's original approach again. Everything which was nomically and/or analytically nested into the information of a signal was also part of the information of that signal. In a fully deterministic world, every signal would then convey no information at all, since there was no alternative to the signal occurring the way it occurred (just like no logical truth and no natural law was considered having informational content). But even if our world were deterministic (which we shouldn't exclude on the basis of a theory of information alone), signals still would carry information for us, since we are largely ignorant of the nomical, analytical, and natural nesting relations that obtain between the headline of this morning's *Washington Post* and everything else that ever happened or will happen in the universe.

The approach is *pragmatic* in the sense that it puts no limits on the ignorance of a subject. It models what some ignorant person may learn by gaining information (i.e. by explicitly excluding worlds, even impossible ones). This cannot model non-circularly the amount of information in logical truths though, since we needed a speaker independent modeling that has no recourse in its definition of *normality* (of worlds) to the logical truths themselves. Thus we can say that the approach models *subjective* possibilities and subjective information gain.

Further Developing Information Flow

In their review of Barwise/Seligman's 1997 book on information flow, David Israel and Johan van Benthem characterize the state of information theory in the following way. With the 70s two different traditions in the field of information theory began to develop, one arising from Paul Grice's logic of conversation with Stalnaker as the key conceptualizer. This tradition was mainly interested in the information-transfer aspects of communication and the dynamics involved. The other tradition, Humean in spirit and having Dretske as their key conceptualizer, was more interested in the link of information with knowledge and the way in which one part of the world could carry information about another part of the world, thus less interested and quiet about the dynamics of information gathering.

The theory of information that we have followed so far in this book belongs mainly to the second camp and even Barwise/Seligman 1997 belongs clearly here. Nevertheless, Barwise's attempt to model the dynamics of epistemic possibilities in the information flow framework can be seen as a way to meet the conceptual challenge described by Israel and van Benthem.

Further Reading

The moderate modal realism we discussed is developed in

📖 Robert Stalnaker, *Inquiry*, Cambridge 1981.

The pragmatic theory of possibility is developed in an information flow framework in

📖 Jon Barwise, 'Information and Impossibilities', *Notre Dame Journal of Formal Logic* 38 (1997), 488-515.

Although Barwise's idea seems quite attractive, there are few discussioin of it yet. You can find a rather detailed discussion that covers a very similar ground as we do in:

📖 Philipp Keller, *Information Flow*, Logics for the (r)age of information, http://www.unige.ch/lettres/philo/enseignants/philipp/research/info.pdf.

5|4   Genetic Information?

One area in which we usually talk of 'information' is genetics. We talk about the genetic *code* as containing *genetic information*. What is that supposed to mean? Is it only a metaphor, or is there more to it? In this chapter we introduce you to a kind of information theoretic perspective on genetics and cellular development. We follow closely some ideas of Douglas Hofstadter. This description is empirically inadequate as an account of replication of genes and carriage of information. The mechanisms of heredity turned out to be more complicated than they were considered in the early 80s. Even by missing the true story, however, we hope to develop a perspective that could be developed into a more complicated, more appropriate information theoretic model of genetic information.

To model genetic information and to highlight the appropriateness of talking of a genetic code Hofstadter invents the game of *Typogenetics*. We start with four letters: A, C, G, T. Arbitrary sequences of them are called 'strands'. These strands play the role of DNA pieces. The letters 'A', 'C', 'G', 'T' model the bases which we find in DNA molecules. Each strand consists of *places* or *units*. For example the strand

(1)   ACGGTTA

consists of seven units, the second of which is occupied by a 'C'. Strands are to be operated upon. We could, for example, lengthen the strand given by attaching further units. A strand can also be copied or cut in two. Operations to be performed on a strand come in a package (like a program to be executed on some input). The little 'machines' that realize these operations by moving along the string are the *typographical enzymes*. They realize the operations by working on one unit at a time, like a Turing machine reading one input under its head. For that moment their operation is bound to that unit. Typographical enzymes are not universal in that each of them starts out at a specific unit, i.e. a particular letter. Given our four letters we have, therefore, four types of enzymes.

Example

Say an enzyme is bound to an 'A'. Its program consists of the following operations:

(i)   delete the unit bound to and move one to the right

(ii) insert a 'C' to the right of this unit

(iii) move one to the right and bind there.

Given the input 'ATTAC' this enzyme will produce the strand 'TCTAC'. If any enzyme moves off the end of the strand it quits its work.

'A' and 'G' form a group called 'purines', 'C' and 'T' a group called 'pyrimidines'. This grouping allows for more general instructions like

(2)   Replace the nearest purine by a pyrimidine

(3)   Cut the strand after the second purine!

Instruction (2) could transform 'ATTAC' into either 'CTTAC' or 'TTTAC'. Typographical enzymes are non-deterministic machines. The instructions are taken here as context free (having the same meaning in all program contexts).

Copying is not done by making another 'ATTAC' from 'ATTAC' like on a Xerox-machine. The enzyme copies 'A' into 'T' (and vice versa), and 'C' into 'G' (and vice versa). So one of the purines is copied into one of the pyrimidines, and vice versa. This is *complementary base pairing*. The strand 'ATTAC' would be copied into 'TAATG'. The enzyme produces a complementary strand from a given strand. The new strand is attached to the original strand (here, we simply write it above it). The copy mode of the enzyme is *On* as long as it is not turned off or the enzyme has walked off the strand.

GENETIC INFORMATION?

Example

Suppose an enzyme attaching to an A has the following program:

(i) Search for the nearest pyrimidine to the right of this unit!

(ii) Start Copying!

(iii) If you hit on a purine, cut the strand here (i.e. to the right of the last pyrimidine).

If this enzyme operates on the following strand

(4)   ACTAGATTCTCCCTTCATGA

it could attach to each of the 'A's. Suppose it starts working at the second 'A'. It goes to the right (crossing the 'G') until it finds a 'T' or a 'C'; starting with the second 'T' in the strand it goes into copy mode until it hits on the third 'A'; here it cuts the strand, so we get:

AAGAGGGAAG
↑
(5)   ACTAGATTCTCCCTTC ✄ ATGA

Separating the attached copied part we arrive at three new strands. There are fifteen commands available:

cut	cut strand(s) [i.e. either the input or the copy as well]
del	delete from the strand (at position)
swi	switch enzyme to the other strand (i.e. the copy)
mvr	move one unit to the right
mvl	move one unit to the left
cop-	turn on Copy mode
off	turn off Copy mode
ina	insert 'A' (to the right)
inc	insert 'C'
ing	insert 'G'

int	insert 'T'
rpy-	search for nearest pyrimidine to the right
rpu-	search for nearest purine to the right
lpy	search for nearest pyrimidine to the left
lpu	search for nearest purine to the left

Each instruction has a three letter abbreviation. They are called 'amino acids'. Thus every enzyme is made up of a sequence of amino acids, like a program consists of lines of code. Now the interesting point in genetics is that we do not start with given enzymes, but we can translate a strand of purines and pyrimidines into enzymes. That is: The strands code for enzymes. Since we considered the strands as inputs for programs (the enzymes), we see that we store the programs in the same place where we store the strands – as it is in a von Neumann digital universal computer. In Typogenetics the data (i.e. the DNA-strands as modelled here) dictate the way they are to be processed. And by this they dictate which strands are produced from them! This, of course, involves a *coding* of the operations in the strands. Pairs of units, called 'duplets', code some amino acid. Given 4 bases we have $4^2 = 16$ duplets. The code is given by the following grid:

first/second base	A	C	G	T
A		cut s	del s	swi r
C	mvr s	mvl s	cop r	off l
G	ina s	inc r	ing r	int l
T	rpy r	rpu l	lpy l	lpu l

Note that an 'AA' codes for nothing. In fact it works as a punctuation mark. If an 'AA' occurs within a strand with the first 'A' on an odd position what is left to this 'AA' codes for one enzyme and if there comes something to the right of it, it codes for another enzyme (do not confuse the punctuation in 'AGCTAAGTCC' with the mere occurrence of an AA in 'AGCAAT').

A *gene* is a part of a DNA strand that codes for an enzyme. A gene is a specification of a program. Since there is a punctuation mark, a single DNA strand can consists of several genes. A DNA strand can be considered to be a batch of programs. Note also that a strand that consists of an odd number of bases contains a last base that codes for nothing. With respect to information theoretic talk about genetics we have, thereby, justified the talk of *genetic code*. (The actual coding of amino acids by bases is, of course, more complicated than the grid given.) In information theory one could even use a more abstract notion of a *gene*: Since a piece of DNA strand might code for more than one gene (by having enzymes attached to different starting points of it) and some phenotype might be yielded by more than one strand, an *abstract gene* might be the genetic information that codes for some feature of the phenotype, where this information might be realized in different substrata (i.e. different strands of duplets). What is preserved even in minor mutation is this abstract genetic information.

The additional letters 's', 'r', 'l' in the grid determine the enzyme's binding preference (which letter they stick to) by determining how the enzyme folds up in space. 's' codes for straight lining, 'r' for a right turn and 'l' for a left turn. The turns in the enzyme can be pictured by arrows: $\Uparrow \Rightarrow \Downarrow \Leftarrow$.

Example
The strand

(6)   TAGATCCAGTCCACATCGA

can be parsed into

(7)   TA GA TC CA GT CC AC AT CG A

with the last A coding for nothing. The translation is:

(8)   rpy r – ina s – rpu l – mvr s – int l – mvl s – cut s – swi r – cop r

the spatial structure of the enzyme enfolds like this:

```
cop
⇑
swi ⇐ cut ⇐ mvl ⇐ int
                    ⇑
                   mvr
                    ⇑
        rpy ⇒ ina ⇒ rpu
```

If we look at the direction of the first and the last segment we can code the binding preference of this enzyme by another grid:

First Segment	Last Segment	Binding-letter
⇒	⇒	A
⇒	⇑	C
⇒	⇐	G
⇒	⇐	T

(Once again, the actual derivation of the spatial structure from the genetic code is much more complicated.)

For all this to work we need a mechanism extracting the information from the gene and building the corresponding enzyme. The machine that does that is a *ribosome*. Strands translate by the work of ribosomes into enzymes, which by typographical engineering produce new strands. In fact the ribosome is the focal point of *information flow* in the whole picture: An enzyme being a translation of a strand contains *the same information* as the strand (only in the form of amino acids, not in the form of bases). The Xerox-principle (see Chapter 3|1) applies in full force: If a DNA strand codes for an enzyme (i.e. contains that information) and the enzyme's code produces a new DNA strand (i.e. contains – by the structure of its program, given its binding preference and typical input – that information), then the original gene contains the information of the produced DNA strand. The ribosome *channels* information from a gene into an enzyme. The enzyme can create new information by building new DNA strands. The actual mechanism in a cell employs messenger RNA to get genetic information from the nucleus to the ribosomes in the cytoplasm. Information is *carried* by the RNA to the ribosomes (by having some special enzymes in the nucleus copying DNA strands in the nucleus into RNA strands).

Enzymes and ribosomes do not care about information. They do, of course, not understand what they are doing. The little typographic machines are only moving along a strand executing one operation at a time. The information is objectively processed by the whole system. It is *there* in the code and exhibited by the structure of the system.

Seen from an adaptionist's perspective one could even say that the gene itself channels information. It channels information from the environment which phenotype traits are able to sustain their bearer and which are not. Thinking of various trade-offs between phenotype traits, their variation by mutation and the accidents of a creature's environment, however, makes one suspect that a principle like the Xerox-principle will fail in this adaptionist channelling.

Self-replication means that a strand of DNA is used to manufacture enzymes which by operating on this strand of DNA in the copy mode produce another instance of that very strand. Information, therefore, can be copied by the cell in the usual sense of copying (i.e. keeping the way of rendering the information).

The information present in the genes determines – given a hierarchy of information extracting devices and development – the phenotype of an organism. Given some measure of length of a gene one could try to measure the information present in a gene either in the syntactic style of Shannon or even in the sense of Algorithmic Information Theory, taking the informational content of some feature of an organism to be the length or measure of the shortest DNA code that determines it. This looks like being a naïve picture of isolating single DNA strands and isolated developments, but some biologists do just that (cf. Haken/Haken-Krell 1989). One might consider the distribution of the bases or duplets within a DNA strand. If they are not equally frequent the occurrence of some base or duplet carries – according to Shannon's measure of information (see Chapter 1|2) – more information than the occurrence of some more frequent base or duplet. Given equal distribution of the genes coding for one of the 20 amino acids involved in DNA reproduction one would carry the information $\log 20 = 4,3$ bits. Given some assessment of ordinary distribution of bases or duplets you can measure the syntactic amount of information of a DNA strand by the sum of its letters/duplets weighted by some given probability measure of their chance of occurring. The DNA of a typical mammal cell contains 3×10^9 duplets, about 50% of which are redundant! The amount of information of a mammal cell measured thus is said to be 6×10^7 bits (cf. Haken/Haken-Krell 1989, 67-68). One can then relate the amount of information present to the size of the memory, arriving thus at a measure of information density in genetic information storage. *E. coli* is said to have an information density of 10^{27} bits/m³.

Second Thoughts

So far there does not seem to be a problem in applying information terminology to biological phenomena. However, having a look at the lively debate on the concept of information in biology that evolved recently in the philosophy of science, it might seem that we have so far only considered a very simplified or even naïve picture of the situation. Well, what is at issue?

It is not really quite clear what is at issue. If biologists use the word 'information', 'meaning', 'genetic code' without talking past each other, there is no reason for a philosopher to intervene. The best thing he might do is to tell them that their concept does not, however, match the concept normal folks have. Chromoquantumdynamics talks about quarks being blue or red, but in fact these are not the kind of things that have any colors in the normal sense of the word (quarks are smaller than the wavelength of visible light). To highlight this might help people outside physics to understand better what the physicists are talking about and might reduce confusions.

To prove a claim like this when it comes to 'information' is of course hopeless, given that there is no one folk-notion of information as you might have grasped by now. On the other hand, showing that a biologist does not use 'information' according to, say, Shannon's explication of it, does not prove that the biologist made any mistake either, but rather that Shannon's theory does not cover all uses of 'information' in science (as you should have grasped by now, too). So what is really at issue?

One discussion seems to center around the question of whether it can reasonably be distinguished between the developmental contributions of genetic causal factors and non-genetic causal factors. Some seem to argue that there is a naturalistic (scientifically respectable) notion of information that can support such a distinction and hence mark a difference between genetic factors and the rest in developmental systems theory. This, however interesting it may be, does not affect the question of whether or not it is correct to use information-vocabulary when talking about the genetic code. It seems that even if, as some advocates of developmental systems theory hold, there is no principled distinction between genetic and non-genetic factors that could be cashed out in information vocabulary, you can still talk about the genetic code as carrying information, as long as you are also willing to apply this terminology to non-genetic causal factors. Whether the parity thesis is true or not is largely an empirical question. We will not pursue this here. If you are interested in this discussion, read the paper by John Maynard Smith from the Further Reading-section.

Quite another question is whether information talk is correct when applied to genes (the way we did above). What are the worries here?

1.) One worry is that it is unclear what the gene codes for. Does it – for example – only code for proteins or does it code for penicillin resistance, if the protein produced has a key role in producing this resistance.

2.) Another worry is that the DNA does not seem to carry indicative but rather imperative semantic content, it carries instructions. But it is unclear how 'carrying information'-talk can be applied to imperatives.

3.) A question closely connected to the problem we briefly discussed above is the parity of information channels. It seems that the symbol carries information about the channel, if the source is known. But then it is arbitrary what the channel is and what the role of the source plays. In biology is no such arbitrariness, therefore information talk is not adequate. Genes code for phenotypes, but phenotypes do not code for genes. The concept of information does not allow such an asymmetry.

4.) Part of the DNA seems to be meaningless; normally we would not think that something containing a message or carrying information carries huge meaningless parts.

Concerning question (1.), the model presented sees the genetic code as primarily coding for proteins. The point of this modelling was to show that the concept of information as presented in this book is abstract enough to cover a sensible talk of genetic information. That the environment is a crucial condition only in correlation with which the genetic code then can be considered to code for the phenotype is no problem for our concept of information, since information is out there in the world (so is there in the environmental conditions as well as in the genetic code proper). Concerning the coding of the proteins the genetic code is not just described in a vague analogy (using merely the vocabulary of information theory) as carrying information, the abstract concept of information directly applies to it. If more of the development of organisms can be described in information terms the better.

Concerning question (2.), the model presented takes the code as coding for imperatives of an imperative programming language, where the effects of executing these imperatives result in structures that are thus indirectly coded for.

Concerning question (3.), the model presented here has no problem with a wider application of information talk, and a choice of different focus according to your explanatory goal in question. The possibility to switch the focus shows that we are dealing with a distributed system that allows reasoning from one part to the other.

Concerning question (4.) it suffices to remember MCT and the occurence of redundancy in code.

Further Reading

The account given in the first part of the chapter draws heavily on Chapter 26 of

- Douglas Hofstadter, *Gödel, Escher, Bach. An Eternal Golden Braid*, London 1979.

The biological details you may find in a textbook on genetics. For the broader picture on evolution and the role of information there, see:

- Daniel Dennett, *Darwin's Dangerous Idea. Evolution and the Meanings of Life*, London 1995.

The part of this chapter titled 'Second Thoughts' refers to a discussion that evolved around a paper by the biologist John Maynard Smith:

- John Maynard Smith, 'The Concept of Information in Biology', *Philosophy of Science* 67, 177-194. (See also the contributions by Godfrey-Smith, Sterelny, and Sarkar, as well as the reply by Smith in the same volume).

For a rather critical view on the use of the concept of information in biology, see

- Paul E. Griffith, 'Genetic Information: A Metaphor in Search of a Theory', *Philosophy of Science* 68, 394-412.

and

- Peter Godfrey-Smith, 'Genes and Codes: Lessons from the Philosophy of Mind?', in: Valerie Gray Hardcastle (ed.), *Where Biology Meets Psychology*, MIT Press 1999, 305-331.

Epilogue

You have come a long way. What have we seen? The theory of information is no unified field of research or framework of reference. The ubiquity of the concept of information in the 'age of information' stands in marked contrast to this vagueness of the very central concept. Whereas in engineering and some scientific contexts (as concerning the transfer of data in bits) the syntactic theory in the vain of Shannon is widely known and the preferred theory referred to, the *common sense* concept of information is related to meaning. According to this predominant view something carries information given some shared convention or regularity between the sender and the receiver. The information thus conveyed can be stated by a sentence. This applies as well to most if not all data base entries.

The classic syntactic approach, however, turns out to contain only partially this intuition. Given some prearranged specific coding some transferred signal can indeed convey information *about* something, but this is relative to the situation, the prearranged coding and the channel used.

The early possible worlds semantic approach gives formal expression to the idea that sentences conventionally contain information. It sustains the relation between meaning and information.

This idea is taken up in a way by situation semantics. Situation semantics provides both an account of linguistic information carriage as well as an account of information being in the world and being conveyed by non-linguistic regularities. The idea of amount of information is – at least for the beginning – given up, but may have been not that central in the first place. That some sentence is more informative than another can in many cases be seen by its logical complexity and the corresponding set of consequences within some theory and using some logic. A logarithmic measure is too far off from the available and practically usable knowledge in situations of communication.

In situation semantics the central notion of an infon can be employed both as the content of a sentence as well as a state of the world, a fact, that information is conveyed of by another event in the world. Therefore we focus on situation theory as the preferred theory of information. Within its framework – especially by its concepts of infons, constraints and infomorphisms – it is possible to outline a theory of semantic information channels and the information architectures used in information flow.

Situation semantics has been classified as a degenerating research program, especially since the untimely death of Jon Barwise. This may be so in semantics, if situation semantics was ever a serious contender to replace truth conditional semantics (ala Davidson) or categorical grammars (ala Montague) or the mentalist framework (ala Fodor or Jackendoff). We believe, however, that this is not so in information theory.

 The idea of infons and their constraints building up an information architecture accounting for information flow may be the basis for a comprehensive theory of information.

 It is further on in intimate connection to externalist accounts of information and the availability of information to cognitive systems in epistemology (in like Dretske's theory of knowledge).

 Its framework is abstract enough to rephrase the idea of genetic information in its terminology.

It is here that a general theory of information and its formal presentation may develop and to its basic ideas we hope to have introduced you.

Further References

This bibliography just gives the references of texts referred to which do not belong to the 'Further Reading' category, but where mentioned in discussion.

Aczél, J. / Daróczy, Z. (1975), *On Measures of Information and their Characterizations*, London.
Bar-Hillel, Yehoshua (1964), *Language and Information. Selected Essays on their theory and application*, Reading/MA.
Bremer, Manuel (1993), *Epistemische und logische Aspekte des semantischen Regelfolgens*, Aachen.
Brillouin, L. (1951), 'Maxwell's Demon Cannot Operate. Information and Entropy I', *J. Appl. Phys.* 22, 334-337.
 – (1962), *Science and Information Theory*, New York.
Cann, Ronnie (1993), *Formal Semantics. An Introduction*, Cambridge.
Carnap, Rudolf (1947/1988), *Meaning and Necessity. A Study in Semantics and Modal Logic*, Chicago.
 – (1950/1967), *Logical Foundations of Probability*, London.
 – (1955), 'Meaning and Synonymity in Natural Languages', *Philosophical Studies* 7, 33-47.
 – (1963), 'Intellectual Autobiography', in: P. A. Schilpp, *The Philosophy of Rudolf Carnap*, London, 3-84.
 – (1977), *Two Essays on Entropy*, Berkeley.
Carnap, Rudolf / Bar-Hillel, Yehoshua (1952/1964). 'An Outline of a Theory of Semantic Information', in: Bar-Hillel 1964, 221-274.
Cherry, E. Collin (1952). 'The Communication of Information', *American Scientist*, 40, 640-664.
Dowe, Phil (manuscript), *Backwards Causation*, http://www.uq.edu.au/~uqpdowe/Research/pdfs/Backwards_Causation.pdf

Fodor, Jerry (1987), *Psychosemantics*, Cambridge/MA.
- (1994), *The Elm and the Expert. Mentalese and its Semantics*, Cambridge/MA.
Gettier, P. (1963), 'Is Justified True Belief Knowledge?', *Analysis*, 23, 121-123.
Haken, Hermann/Haken-Krell, Maria (1989), *Enstehung von biologischer Information und Ordnung*, Darmstadt.
Hartley, R. V. L. (1928), 'Transmission of Information', *The Bell System Technical Journal* VII, 535-563.
Hegel, G. W. F. (1832/1985), *Wissenschaft der Logik* (Gesammelte Werke, vol. 21), Hamburg.
Jackendoff, Ray (1985), 'Information is in the Mind of the Beholder', *Linguistics and Philosophy* 8, 23-33.
- (1997), *The Architecture of the Language Faculty*.
Khinchin, A. I. (1957), *Mathematical Foundations of Information Theory*, New York.
Krauth, L. (1970/1997), *Die Philosophie Carnaps*, Wien.
Lewis, David (1986), *On the Plurality of Worlds*, London.
Maxwell, James Clerk (1871), *Theory of Heat*, London.
Montague, Richard (1974), *Formal Philosophy*, New Haven/London.
Mormann, Thomas (2000), *Rudolf Carnap*, München.
Nyquist, H. (1924), 'Certain Factors Affecting Telegraph Speed', *The Bell System Technical Journal* III, 324-346.
O'Leary-Hawthorne, John (1996), 'The Epistemology of Possible Worlds: A Guided Tour', *Philosophical Studies* 84, 183-202.
Rodd, P. (1963), 'Some Comments on Entropy and Information', *Am. J. Phys.* 32, 333-335.
Schneider, T. (2003), *Information Theory Primer*, version 2.54, ftp://ftp.ncifcrf.gov/pub/delila/primer.ps.
Shannon, C. E. (1938/1993), 'A Symbolic Analysis of Relay and Switching Circuits', in: C. E. Shannon, *Collected Papers*, New York, 471-495.
- (1948/1993), 'The Mathematical Theory of Communication', in: C. E. Shannon, *Collected Papers*, New York, 5-83.
Spinoza, B. (1674/1925), *Spinoza Opera*, vol. IV, Heidelberg.

van Bentham, Jeremy (1979), 'What is Dialectical Logic?', *Erkenntnis* 14, 333-47.
von Neumann, John (1955), *Mathematical Foundations of Quantum Mechanics*, Princeton.
Wiener, Norbert (1948), *Cybernetics or Control and Communication in the Animal and the Machine*, MIT.

Glossary of Notation

$\log_2$, log	natural logarithm to the base 2, if not otherwise indicated.
$\sum_{i=1}^{n} p_i$	sum of all $p_1, p_2, ..., p_n$.
p_k, $p(k)$	unconditional probability of k.
p_{kl}, $p_k(l)$, $P(l\|k)$	conditional probability of l, given k.
$p(l, k)$	unconditional probability of l and k.
$\lim_{T \to \infty}$	taking the limit.
min	minimum
lg	length
$\equiv$	material biconditional
$\supset$	material conditional
$\neg$	negation
$\wedge$	conjunction
$\vee$	disjunction
$\forall$	universal quantifier
$\exists$	existential quantifier
$\to$	metalanguage conditional; relevant conditional in chapter 5|2
$s \models A$	s makes A true
$s \not\models A$	s does not make true A
$\Gamma, \Lambda, \Sigma, ...$	sets of types or statements
φ, ψ	propositional variables (if not indicated otherwise)
$\Gamma \vdash A$	A can be derived from Γ
$\bot$	falsum
$\{x\|F(x)\}$	the set of all x such that x is F

GLOSSARY OF NOTATION

$x \in A$	x is a member of A
$s_1 \subseteq s_2$	s_1 is a subset of s_2
$\Box A$	necessary A
$\Diamond A$	possibly A
$[x^* \mid s \models I]$	type abstraction
$\Rightarrow$	constraint, metalanguage conditional in chapter 5|3
$\Leftrightarrow$	metalanguage biconditional in chapter 5|3

www.ingramcontent.com/pod-product-compliance
Lightning Source LLC
Chambersburg PA
CBHW061128010526
44116CB00023B/2999